Indigo

Indigo

Arm Wrestling, Snake Saving, and
Some Things in Between

Padgett Powell

Catapult
New York

ISBN: 978-1-64622-005-2

Cover design by Jaya Miceli
Book design by Wah-Ming Chang

Library of Congress Control Number: 2020932500

Catapult
1140 Broadway, Suite 706
New York, NY 10001

Printed in the United States of America
10 9 8 7 6 5 4 3 2 1

Contents

Foreword

The sign of a true writer is that his stories are your stories.

One day she's there, of a piece, as they say, all the moods and curves and scents, the comfortable fit, the heat that comes off her body at night—she's a little furnace over there and always has been. *No wonder,* I go. *No wonder you wake up cold.*

Time moves the way it does, and one morning I lie in bed listening to her in the kitchen making coffee, and know something is missing. Maybe has been for a while. I don't know a better way to explain it, one morning I know there's a little less of her there. It is sudden enough, this first morning, that it's possible it's not her, that something has gone wrong with me—things have gone wrong suddenly before. The feeling comes back a week later, and a week after that. An erosion, sometimes in little pieces, sometimes in whole blocks. We make an appointment to see the doctor, and at the last minute she calls it off.

I work most afternoons in a small cabin-like house next to the house where we live, and lately, often as not, I can't find her when I get back. I have learned to look first down by the tiny red shack in the meadow, maybe two hundred yards from the house, where she sometimes sits on the steps, thinking. The place is full of old newspapers and baby spiders.

Pretty soon I am spending nights in a chair by the front door, and the world runs in pauses and spurts as it will sometimes do when you are stricken for sleep. Tonight I startle awake, dreaming of freezing to death in Lake Michigan. The door is wide open, twelve thirty at night, creaking noises as it blows open and shut. I drive every road in a five-mile radius that night and do not get her back until sometime after two. It is the sheriff's department that finds her, and she comes back into the house barefoot and freezing cold, shaking, her feet stark white.

By now time means next to nothing. Night and day are interchangeable, the days of the week, even seasons. Some nights she won't eat, one evening she rolls up a copy of *Sports Illustrated* and, thinking it's a knife, stabs me in the hallway. She forgets how to make coffee. She hasn't started a day without coffee ten times in forty years.

As the new coffee cook, I am going through a pound of Starbucks every four days. I scald myself most mornings, and once I watch what I have made eat a hole through the coffee filter. I think maybe I'm not adding enough water. That same morning, without any particular warning, she is in tears. Is somebody dead? Has she killed someone in the night?

I hold her a little while, as long as she'll let me hold her. "You never killed anybody. Who would you kill?"

"You know," she says, "him."

Twenty minutes later, coffee grounds sticking to her chin, she is happy and relieved—guiltless—almost herself again, headed out the door to fill the bird feeders, and it is in that moment of calm, when things are better, that I know it's all gone.

She has to be tricked into the place where she'll die, and she knows what she's there to do. An unbelievable betrayal, the reasons are worthless, they make sense but no difference.

Seven months is all that's left, a little more. Three visits to the emergency room in the first few weeks. Twenty stitches across her eye, swollen shut. Seven falls in six days, a wheelchair. A hundred and forty miles, round-trip, every day, sometimes twice. She only picks at the food I bring, picks in the beginning and then she barely eats at all, turning her head away from the spoon. It has been a while now since she's been able to feed herself. Her face has narrowed and her eyes seem enormous and dark. Someone else's eyes, newborn, not a memory left.

The call comes at three in the morning, and she's gone. I knew it was coming that night, the hospice people offered to put another bed in her room. And I couldn't. In all my life, I've never let even my dogs go like this—ten, twelve dogs, I've held every one of them at the end. And I can't really say if it matters that she doesn't know who I am, or even who she is. Probably not, at least to her. But does it matter that I wasn't there? The same question, day after day. And even knowing there is nothing for me in an answer, it's somehow still all that matters.

The death certificate says sixty-three pounds. And that is what it looked like, about sixty-three pounds.

It rolls in like the fog, but not on little cat's feet. The kind of fog where you're never quite sure of the distance. Nothing is defined. Friends empty her closets, folding and boxing every sweater and coat and pair of pants like it was all going back where it came from, under the Christmas tree. I give away two thousand books to the Whidbey Island animal rescue society, and my old truck goes to my brother's dog. The dog rides around shotgun, jiggling his tongue at the unaltered females of Billings, Montana. I smile at that, Tom and his dog haunting the streets of Billings in a fourteen-year-old sun-faded Honda Ridgeline—original leather, moonroof, and its famous hidden trunk, located under the truck bed. I say goodbye to the truck, pleased that my brother is pleased—it turns out that giving stuff away agrees with me.

Still, nothing is completely gone because you give it away. I'd owned the Ridgeline two years when the noises began. Still under warranty. I'd turn the engine over and in fifteen seconds the noises would start, frog-like noises from the back seat. If you want to hear the sound for yourself, put your fingers in your ears and clear your throat.

The service-department lady at Honda did not care for my attitude. I sometimes wonder if there is someone out there who looks like me doing terrible things and I keep running into the victims. The woman would not try putting her fingers in her ears and said if I couldn't replicate the noise, she obviously couldn't fix the problem. So, a hoax. Fair enough, I've been caught. I can't help myself, I just have to sit around in car dealerships for an hour and fifteen minutes with ghost symptoms. "Larry, line two" is music to my ears. In fact, it and leg surgery are my hobbies. The dealership lady called the service manager, who did put his fingers in his ears and said it sounded like a suspension problem. Two hours later, I got the car back, but the suspension wasn't it. The lady was more polite this time. She said, "Well, if it happens again . . . ," etc., and then: "At least you got a free car wash." Three hours and fifteen minutes to get a free car wash, why didn't I think of this sooner?

I take the Ridgeline to Dana Gildersleeve, whose Whidbey Tire & Auto was the best car repair shop on the island, especially taking into consideration the barbershop mien of the waiting area, and in one minute Dana has the situation under control. He opens the hidden trunk, revealing a little tribe of neon green frogs living in apparent harmony around the spare tire. Harmony in the first sense of the word, where but for lack of a tenor, the frogs could take the act on the road.

For many years before I gave the truck to Tom's dog, it was used mostly on weekends, hauling the garbage to the dump, and for many years the maggots fell off the garbage bags, and into the hidden trunk, and the frogs never ran out of food. Still, in the end they disappeared, I don't know why but it wasn't starvation. Maybe they found a quieter truck, but for as long as they were in my care I kept an eye on them, and kept them fat and tame. I still sometimes see a blue Ridgeline on the road and conjure up the old gang sitting around the spare. This also makes me smile. I am turning into a grinning machine.

Meanwhile, stuff continues to disappear, mostly to Good Cheer, and when enough of it is gone I pack up what is left and head for South Dakota. To teach. And suddenly my life is filling up with things that are nothing to do with what they are called. Good Cheer, forewords, introductions, Creative Writing, Fine Arts, the Critical Tract of Graduate Studies. How this bodes for the teaching business, I can't say. In any case, I leave the island and point the Penske moving van east. Mrs. Dexter's ashes ride up in front.

To get to South Dakota from Whidbey Island, turn right off the ferry to State Route 525, right again to the interstate, and follow that till you freeze your nuts off. That's the Black Hills, more or less. Another day, until your nuts factually click together when you walk, like you've got snooker balls in your pocket, and you're in Vermillion. And the University of South Dakota. We like to think of ourselves as the Harvard of . . . a minute, here . . . of South Dakota, the Harvard of South Dakota.

Academia, a desk, a parking sticker, a title: *Writer in Residence, Weather Permitting.* Or, as Padgett puts it, the world. He can call it the world now that he's out of it for good. He was at the University of Florida for thirty-five years, give or take. Thirty-five is a lot of years and if your goal in life is to see Padgett Powell cheerful, go to Florida and ask him about the good writers he turned out. He is not as cheerful about his own stuff. Go figure.

It is not impossible that you are wondering by now, *Where's my damn foreword?* I know I would be. The answer is, what I am forewording is not so much this particular book but the possibilities when a live brain stumbles across spectacular writing, and for this I am drawn back to the title story of the second collection of stories by another spectacular writer, Flannery O'Connor. Her collection was called *Everything That Rises Must Converge*, and with the exception of a few of Robert Frost's poems, it was the first consequential writing I ever read. I was a long time figuring out what that title meant.

In any case, the story and the title are still there in my head, along with Flannery O'Connor's other stories—and along with Robert Frost—and other spectacular voices I have stumbled across on the long road to academia. There are maybe ten or twelve in all and one of them of course belongs to Padgett Powell. It is perhaps my own spectacularly good idea to resist naming the others.

A quick story about comparing writers:

This was a few years ago, don't ask me when. I got a call from Esther Newberg's assistant. Esther is a literary agent, but it doesn't hurt to be careful about that *my agent* stuff, just on the off chance some soldier of the ever-fickle new correctness decides it's insensitive. For the record, Esther is not mine, and I am not hers. Unless she says I am.

So. Esther's assistant says she has some excellent news,

although I know enough about the way things work that if it were really excellent news I would be talking to Esther herself. As far as I can tell, she lost interest a long time ago in making money, at least for herself. She is that rarest kind of agent who has reached a place in life where it is no longer necessary to keep score. I only hope saying this doesn't get her shunned out of the agents' club, but then she has probably had showdowns with every publisher in the world and as far as I know there is nobody left in New York to intimidate, so what does a girl do for fun? The answer is that she goes to some ranch in Arizona where they torture you for two weeks, feed you nuts and berries, pair you up with a horse, wake you up before five for sit-ups, etc., and it feels so good when they stop, New York looks tickled pink to have you back. What else? Well, she likes being the one who bears good tidings, and from what I've seen of agents and cities, there are worse things you can turn out to be.

But the assistant. Esther's assistants are lovable, always lovable, they always sound glad to hear my voice. My suspicion is that they get paid to be nice, where with Esther—how to put it?—I am one of her boys, and I think she likes me. Meaning I am very likely the only American alive who calls New York City for cheering up. But this time Esther is not in New York but on a borrowed horse, back in Arizona, so the assistant is calling to let me know about the prize, a prestigious prize. Yes, I know this is straight out of *A Christmas Story*, but there is nothing I can do about it. These things are *ordained*.

So I say, What kind of prize?

The answer is, It's from France.

Then she says, "It's very prestigious," and then, in a tone not necessarily meant to be heard, "... or so I have been told." For reasons I am not able to explain, I am afraid to follow the trail of *or so I have been told* back to its source. I will just say that until this afternoon, the only prize I ever heard of in France is the yellow shirt you get to wear for winning yesterday's stage of the Tour de France. Oh, and the trophy that Rafael Nadal bites every time he wins the French Open.

The next day, maybe a week, I call Padgett but he's in Europe and so I speak to his lovely instead. The thought runs through my head that word of the prestigious prize has gotten out. Maybe Padgett has gone to Paris to meet the plane. Maybe he won last year and has been hired to make the presentation speech. How to ask? I go, "So, is this about the prize?"

What are the chances?

Two literary awards from Europe in the same week— my unknown prize, Padgett's unknown prize. Padgett's, however, comes with ten thousand pounds sterling, which is money over there, and the contest buys five thousand copies of the book and distributes them among freshmen students at the University of Edinburgh. Hungry young minds, you might say. With attention spans. Who don't read books because they have to, but because they want to.

My award, as mentioned, is highly prestigious. Prestigious beyond crass monetary rewards. It includes a hotel room for three days and a daily stipend to cover lunch. It is not clear who pays for the plane tickets over.

And this in some odd way is familiar.

If you will indulge me for only a couple more minutes, I'll get to *Indigo*. I promise. But first come back with me a little further, maybe twenty years—the blink of an eye in the history of the world—back before news of literary awards, before Esther was home on the range and Padgett was on his way to Europe. Me, I was at home in my office, looking out the window, feeling queasy. It doesn't take much to get me queasy and never has. A much-loved black Labrador had died that week—the dog belonged to the neighbors, but slept and ate with us. He also ate with the neighbors, and his death was due to the complications of diabetes. I once saw this animal eat the same slab of steak twice in less than a minute. The truth is I loved this animal and could never find it in my heart to barbecue steaks without throwing one on for old Charcoal too, and the incident I am talking about now, he woofed this slab of meat down right off the grill, tossed it back up because it was too hot for his stomach, then ate it again almost before it hit the ground.

So I am standing at the window overlooking Puget Sound, queasy. I have known since the day we moved in, Mrs. Dexter and me, that this is the best house we will ever have, and I remember this scene exactly, notwithstanding the fact that every time I run the math, the years come out all wrong, and not only wasn't I looking out over Puget Sound, I hadn't even heard of Charcoal yet, or the island. Wrong dog, wrong side of America. But these are only details, just the old bean doing those things it does. It probably just wants attention.

Anyhow, the week I am still talking about now, even though I was in Philadelphia—the fourteenth floor of 400 North Broad Street in Philadelphia, Pennsylvania, definitely in Philadelphia—*Time* magazine had printed an article about promising young writers. This, then, is where I first locked horns with Padgett Powell, on the pages of *Time*. As horn-locking goes, it wasn't much of a show. The occasion was each of us had published a first novel. There may have been a couple of other names mentioned, I can't remember. What happened was, I'd written an excellent first paragraph—I still like that paragraph—followed by, well, a first novel. Padgett had written a pretty good first paragraph followed by a novel that I saw compared favorably, maybe in *The Philadelphia Inquirer*, with John Updike and F. Scott Fitzgerald. Specifically, as I remember, with *The Great Gatsby*, which was one of my own favorite novels, being among the handful that I'd ever read. I still like *Gatsby*, but this tendency to praise books because you've read them does you no favors later in life, looking back on all the things you didn't know you didn't know. It explains, for instance, how I once believed Norman Mailer was the cat's nuts, and look how that turned out.

So there are advantages I think to putting off reading until you've been around long enough to understand what things mean, but there are drawbacks too. I remember all this because Mrs. Dexter and I had just that afternoon picked up a seven-week-old golden retriever that cried whenever you put him in his cardboard box, and finally Mrs. Dexter got out of our bed and slept with the puppy, and I sat alone on the edge of the bed on a cold sheet with my heart in my hands, wondering how I was going to break the news that the big plans were off. See, Mrs. Dexter at least half believed me when I said I was going to be a writer and we were going to have an exciting life—Mrs. Dexter and I and the baby that was still a couple of months from coming out, and the future had never looked brighter, but then I have found that the future is never as bright as when *Time* says you have one. At this point I had, as mentioned, read the previously mentioned collection of Flannery O'Connor stories, a book of Robert Frost, and the first seventy pages of *Edisto*, and, not illogically, concluded this was *writing*. Real writers, not newspaper columnists. And my chances of squeezing into that world with those writers were exactly as good as persuading Charcoal to chew steak before he swallowed it.

As for the magazine story itself, the truth is, I don't remember. If you'd asked me last week I'd have said it was in *Newsweek*, and even if there was a third new writer to watch, or a fourth, those writers were only decoration. Not that I wasn't. We were all blooming tulips around the monument, and the monument was the young genius from Florida.

Quite a bit of time passed before I cracked it open again,

Edisto, and then my intention was only to read far enough to find a mistake. What I considered a mistake. Anything bigger than punctuation. An hour went past, another hour. I decided to give it another sixty minutes, and then another half hour, and in this way I finished the book without meaning to.

And now, even if you never get a foreword, you get a revelation: I wasn't jealous.

How to explain? Well, back in 1954, my stepfather, who believed in books, gave in and bought a television set. We were the last family on the block except maybe the Shermans. Don't get me started on the Shermans. The Cleveland Indians and their power-hitting first baseman Vic Wertz were playing the New York Giants in the World Series, and in a country where until recently only one adult in fifty or so had ever seen the greatest athletes of their time play their various games, half of the population saw Willie Mays make the most phenomenal catch—and throw—in World Series history. Millions of people saw the greatest player in the world at his greatest moment. Who but a maniac could be *jealous?*

You might as well be jealous of the moon.

Padgett, of course, was not finished. Beyond writing the best first novel I ever read—still my opinion, even now that I've read a few others—Padgett in some ways only got better. Yes, it's one thing to catch the famous shot off the bat of Vic Wertz on a dead run in the deepest center field of any ballpark in the world, much less the Polo Grounds. It's one thing to do it once, it's something else to keep doing it, or at least being up to doing it again and again. To do it until it's expected, which, through no fault of your own, puts you in the same dugout with John Updike. By way of example, take Padgett's collection of short stories *Aliens of Affection*. To my knowledge—and I am more grown-up these days and many of those two thousand books that I gave away were read— to my knowledge there has never been any book before or after as unhinged and perfectly hung at the same time. *Don Quixote* comes to mind, but I can't say so without risking my reputation in academia.

Still, you try looking for the right tone for the inner life of a personable lunatic/genius and call me when you find it.

But to the job at hand: I need at least to offer Padgett and his publishers a blurb, even if the foreword isn't really turning out to be a foreword. So, a blurb: *The book in your hands is at least tied for the second-best first collection of nonfiction ever collected by an author of the best first novel in history.*

I don't think a word can be said in rebuttal. *Edisto* spawned five more novels and three collections of short stories, and this single collection of magazine pieces, which in its own way may go the deepest of the bunch.

I have given up trying to figure out the critical responses to Padgett's work except to mention that a review is only as good as the critic, and don't get me started on that. The first thing, of course, is that Padgett is easy pickings. If you introduce yourself to the world with a novel like *Edisto,* receive an overwhelming response of the congratulatory kind and comparisons to some of the great writers of the twentieth century, you are suddenly and without your permission in the same foxhole with Updike and maybe Joan Didion. To say that from the day your own book goes out into the world, you are one of them—eloquent, deep, clever, and funny—two different things, by the way, clever and funny, and if anybody offers you the choice, take funny. So *Edisto* is the watermark, for lack of a better word—the expectation. That's an entirely different situation from someone who writes a book just interesting enough to be an afterthought in *Time*'s celebration of Padgett Powell. That person has wiggle room in subsequent books to find his way where Padgett is expected to pick up right where he left off, deep and eloquent and deft, etc., as if that's what's waiting for him in the mirror every morning, ordinary as shoes and socks. And while it is true that very fine writing often looks easy, even passes unnoticed, that doesn't mean it is. There are sweat marks on the armrests, and there are in fact writers who have swapped teeth for stories, and one way or another, trading pain for words is a bargain we/they make all the time. What struggles Padgett goes through to produce his stories, I don't know. They don't necessarily show in the work, but you have to be insensitive—there, I've said it, and I'm not going to apologize—not to understand they are there.

On this subject, more or less, there are only a few things you can get paid for in the writing business more revealing of character than the criticism of other peoples' art, where the opportunity to promote yourself and slip the blade in all at the same time is an art in itself. My own literary criticism is that, so far, whatever Padgett writes, I wish I'd written it too. I had not seen most of these pieces before I was recruited to foreword them, and like the novels and short stories, they leave me stunned.

A while ago I also published a collection of nonfiction. An old friend named Rob Fleder put it together. We had an ideal division of labor. He found the columns—mostly it was columns—and picked which ones we used. He figured out the right order to confront the reader, named the book *Paper Trails*, fought the petty cocksuckers that had bought my old newspaper—the *Daily News*—for the rights to reprint, everything but sold the book door-to-door. Meanwhile, I had a nice time, as they say. It was not unpleasant, going thumbs up, thumbs down on the sampler Fleder put together. This was the first part of Fleder's job, and when it was done I got out of the way and let him finish what he started.

It goes without saying that, as of my first reading of *Indigo*, the sweet taste of *Paper Trails* is not the same. *Indigo* has the same qualities as Padgett's fiction. Unmistakable craft, profundity without even trying. I think, *Why didn't Fleder pick out better stories?* And yes, the stories in *Indigo* are stories, as much as his fiction. They move like stories, carry the same expectations, they end like stories. They do not remind you of newspaper columns. The prose is top-shelf, as always, and when the occasional note comes off-key, this is only the nature of nonfiction. Without the off-notes, you can't trust what you're reading.

As for the pieces themselves, there are no weak sisters. Every one is memorable, full of places and people you know even if you don't know them, and even if you can't always remember which scene goes with which story. The great strength—this because so much of what else is good flows from it—may simply lie in their accuracy. They are dead accurate. This doesn't only mean getting it right, and getting the context right, it has also to do with what things you choose to be right about. A perfect eye, knowing when to talk, when to shut up.

A curious note comes to mind: The things Padgett admires most and even loves are things that don't love him back. Or can't. Again and again, craft trumps affection. This, however, is not necessarily true of the first piece, concerning the world champion super-heavyweight arm wrestler Cleve Dean. It is my guess that Padgett himself sees the title story here, about his hunt to catch and fondle the endangered, beautiful indigo snake, as the star of the show, but for me it's the arm wrestler. Cleve Dean was once the best arm wrestler in the world. In fact, eight years in a row. Then he quit for ten years and ate himself up to 700 pounds or so, where the best medical minds available in Pavo, Georgia, agreed he couldn't walk, even though he could clearly walk, and from that spot in life went back to reclaim what, as far as he was concerned, had always been his. The world title, which, when Padgett picked up the story, was scheduled to be decided in Sweden.

There are warm-up matches in other places that Cleve Dean wins easily, but not so easily that he doesn't strain his arm. Thus sore-armed, aging, and overweight, he arrives in Sweden, the center of attention from the moment he walks into the hotel. Everyone wants pictures, autographs. A strange woman sits in his lap in the hotel lobby. In the group pictures, Cleve is automatically ceded a spot in the middle.

The arm wrestling itself happens on a stage, and only Cleve is allowed to wait on the stage between matches. It is an advantage—because of his weight, coming up and down the stairs exhausts him—but not a word of protest from the other arm wrestlers, who are aware of who is the cash cow—Cleve—and who isn't—them.

Still, malice is loose. A Georgian trainer running around beating his face into a wall, reasons unknown. Arguments, bleeding, money. It is not a manly blood sport where everybody shakes hands at the end and goes home best pals. The Georgians and the Japanese come as teams and huddle together in little armies: uniforms, bodyguards, trainers, always apart, the Georgians sharing some quiet, insulting joke that we don't understand.

And then it's the matches themselves, the super-heavyweights, Cleve and the Georgian champion, Zauri Tskadadze. (A nod here, by the way, to just keeping the two kinds of Georgian arm wrestlers straight—one from Georgia where the ghost of Jimmy Carter's little brother Billy still drives the country roads at night, drinking lukewarm Billy Beer, the other where they drink vodka for breakfast and were once part of the USSR—a nagging complication that would distract a less organized mind to, well, distraction. Reading Padgett's story, you are not aware of the problem.)

The match is over almost before it starts. Cleve is slammed to the table—*flashed*, as it's called—and then, before this news has a chance to settle, it happens again. This second time is not a replay, or part of the game. Perhaps it's celebration to the Georgian, but for Cleve it is humiliation pure and simple, childish, and more than that, an insult. The men's hands are still gripped and Cleve, as unexpectedly as the Georgian's second flash, takes Tskadadze's hand in both of his and slams the Georgian hand in the other direction.

This is also childish.

And perhaps it is worth mentioning that at this level of competition, the muscles and bones and tendons are so close to the tearing/breaking point anyway that what Cleve does might easily have left Tskadadze brushing his teeth left-handed for life. Not that he didn't bring it on himself.

Still, from what I see, this is how Cleve Dean begins coming to terms with disbelief. He is older, overweight, out of shape, his arm is hurt, and it still makes no sense, what has happened. The world has turned on him and taken away what was his by rights and luck and maybe by birth and shows every intention of never giving it back.

And Cleve in turn is saying it doesn't matter, that's what taking Tskadadze down with two hands was all about. What he has done is not just outside the rules of the sport, it is outside its *manners*.

Back in Pavo, Georgia, Cleve comes face-to-face with the

world, and it's not academia. He is damaged, maybe beyond repair. He blames a sore arm, he says he'd like another try at this Zauri Tskadadze. He talks about running for governor. He tells the drive-in teller at the bank that he won everywhere he went, another championship, per usual, and per usual, he's come back the same as he left. Modest, lovable, honest.

And that's really what I've got to say about *Indigo*. It is a beautiful collection of stories. I can barely stand to have it be over, especially to leave Cleve Dean back in Pavo, acting whole and happy in some imitation of the way things were. As if the unpleasantness in Sweden never happened. I did not get to see, and wanted to, more of Cleve and Padgett together, specifically to see Cleve throw his gigantic arm around the writer's shoulders, sizing up the genius from Gainesville, deciding this is a consequential human being that has come to write him up. I would like to have left Padgett on that note, but fondling his indigo isn't bad either, and he is still the best, even if not the best-known, writer of his generation. If these pieces are it, if he never writes another word, there are dozens of scenes in his stuff that will still be lodged in my brain when they take it out at the coroner's office to weigh it.

It is not impossible that I have misjudged the story about Cleve. I have said after all that Padgett has a dead-accurate eye. Maybe he is just reporting human nature. More likely just nature itself, with no particular reference to humans.

Maybe he has only acknowledged, in his own way, what

we have known since our ancestors first came out of the cave hungry. Could be that after all of my bragging about his art, Padgett is a scientist, a human being who has noticed over the years what the whole world knows—that when you're hurt badly enough, nature tells you to hide.

—PETE DEXTER

Indigo

Cleve Dean

Against its reputation as a pastime of drunks, against the notion that it is stupid, arm wrestling does most efficiently what sport is asked to do, which is translate the muddle of success and failure in life into the knowable: who wins and who doesn't and why. In these terms, arm wrestling looks consummately elegant, the locked jaw articulate and the grunting sublime. Your arm, your will, and victory or loss. There is precious little equipment, no brain damage, and you can walk away from it. It is a clear and possibly heroic moment in the smudged, fudged modern world. And if there can be an undisputed world champion in a sport as regionalized and unrecognized and marginalized and fractionated as arm wrestling, Cleve Dean of Pavo, Georgia, was once it and is now, in 1995, at age forty-two, vying to be it again.

Cleve Dean is a farmer and pulp wooder who disappeared from the sport of arm wrestling for nearly ten years after being on top of it for eight. In his absence he ballooned to nearly seven hundred pounds and is thought by some arm wrestlers to have gotten so heavy that he died. He is going to Sweden in a week to try to be champion again, and I am going with him because I want to meet a world champion, of anything, but particularly a world champion who may weigh seven hundred pounds.

When I walk into his house in Georgia—which I have, because he has yelled, "Come on in!"—it is dark and there is something big on the floor that somehow commands my attention. It, like, moves. It's him—Cleve Dean. I judge him to be about five hundred pounds, but I can't tell or know yet how much he weighs. He hardly does himself. I have driven my Chevy truck instead of my wife's Toyota to make a good impression (a man in hogs and logs who at six seven might weigh seven hundred pounds might be a giant redneck shit-ass), and now I have to try to shake hands with this pile of man on the floor in order to keep making a good impression. And I can tell that he is aware it is important for him to show his manners too and that that ordinarily includes standing up when you shake hands, but this is not ordinary. Five hundred pounds getting up just to shake hands?

Cleve Dean's voice is deep and calm, Southern FM quality. His face is boyish under thinning hair. He looks gentle: partly tired and partly ready to be amused. He moves his arm, the famous one, slowly and widely to my approach, offering me the catcher's-mitt-size hand on the long end of a long arm that is one inch shy of being two feet around, and it looks, this arm, like the leg of an ordinary person down there attempting to legwhip me. It is not a steroidy tacky veiny thing but a Michelangelo thing. It looks like big stones under skin.

The hand that Cleve Dean is bringing me is fast and huge. He can punch a digital stopwatch on and off in six hundredths of a second. They told him at the World's Strongest Man Contest he participated in a few years ago that he has the "largest natural bone structure on earth." When you shake this hand, you don't shake it, you shake, at best, a part of it—rather like grabbing a pommel on a saddle when mounting a horse. The thumbhole in Cleve Dean's custom-drilled bowling ball will accommodate a banana.

With two hands Cleve Dean can pick up a five-hundred-pound hog by the ears and set it down gently on the other side of a fence. With one hand he can pick up one end of a twelve-inch-by-twelve-inch-by-sixty-foot heart-pine floor joist and with the other wrap a chain around it and with either hand signal his brother to pull the joist out of the pile of joists with the log truck while he surfs on the joist.

Cleve Dean sits on the floor at the foot of his king-size bed and gets the phone, a Lucite model showing the internal parts and held together with electrical tape. He is calling about his passport, which he needs to go to Sweden. On one side of the bed is an arm-wrestling trainer called a gripper, which looks like a squat rack for a person about eighteen inches tall. A 12-gauge single-shot shotgun leans on the night table. On the night table is a box of shells, two PlenTPaks of Big Red gum, two Big Gulp cups, and a pink ceramic pony.

The night table on the other side of the bed has on it an alarm clock with twin bells on top; a bowl with a fat turquoise candle in it and chewed gum stuck to the rim; a can of Glade Potpourri spray; a Bic pen; a Burger King fries box with cigarette butts in it; an empty Band-Aid wrapper; a used diaper; a book of blank personal checks; an orange Autolite solenoid wire; a coat hanger; a bottle of NyQuil; a pair of thong panties; a crucifix necklace on a gold chain; two arm-wrestling scrapbooks; a bottle of Ralph Lauren cologne on its side; a paperback volume of *Daddy's Girl: The Shocking True Story of a Child's Ordeal of Shame*, by Charlotte Vale Allen, with a lollipop stem in it serving as a bookmark; and, from National Financial Publications of Slidell, Louisiana, "The Complete Guide to Home-Based Employment."

Also on that side of the bed is an arm-wrestling trainer that is a regulation sit-down table fitted with a cable and pulleys for building what is called side pressure, the pressure that moves most directly to the pin pad you want to take your opponent's arm to; there are ninety pounds on the weight sled. The peg you grip with your non-pulling hand is wrapped with an empty Lay's potato-chip bag secured by a woman's elastic hair band. Cleve explains that the peg was hurting his hand. Of the machine itself he says, "That thing right there now, it'll bust your arm down quick."

In 1973, the man with the largest natural bone structure in the world (if you choose not to question the authority of whoever was backstage with the tape and calipers at the World's Strongest Man Contest, where Cleve Dean takes pride in having pulled a 17,500-pound Peterbilt tractor a hundred feet up a slight incline in twenty-nine seconds) secured a tryout with the Miami Dolphins without having played a down of organized football. Despite Don Shula's enthusiasm over Cleve Dean's running the forty faster than a 265-pound man was supposed to, which was as large a man as the NFL had performance profiles for at the time, and over his slinging things around in the weight room, the NFL's strict non-tampering policy with junior college students required a release from Pete Rozelle before the Dolphins could look seriously at him, and getting that took over a year, and by then he had ruptured a disk in his back. He did this joist surfing.

Unable to get into professional athletics, Cleve Dean entered a Columbus, Georgia, arm-wrestling tournament in December 1977 and lost, but in July 1978 in Atlanta he won a national title and went on to so dominate arm wrestling that for a while he made a living on its small purses. He would sometimes be unofficially conceded first place because people would forfeit against him, saving their arms for second-place pulling. Rules were created to thwart his hegemony. These rules Cleve Dean fought by becoming irritable, fighting with referees and competitors and promoters, and this, his "being shitty," as he puts it, was not his style. He even once struck an official in the chest—"Hodhawmighty-knows, they banned me from that association!" In 1986, he quit, eight years after his first appearance on arm wrestling's obscure stage.

He blew up to the life-threatening 700 pounds, was deemed 100 percent disabled ("Technically, I cannot walk. Any doctor will tell you, 'There's no way he can walk'"), and entered a depression proportional to his size. "I never did quit walking," he says, but you get the impression it was close.

From down where he was, he decided, as people do,

to come out of retirement. He loaded a grocery cart with weights and started "pushing that joker" around his garage. "Then I joined the Y. Started riding the robicycle. Doin' water walking. Just kept going." So far he has dropped 250-plus pounds, and as mysteriously as he left the top of the world of arm wrestling in 1986, he is suddenly now back on it. Recently he won the Yukon Jack world title in San Francisco, and now is headed out to Stockholm for the World Armwrestling Federation Championships, his expenses paid for one week of publicity and one week of competition. It is known that his arm may be too sore to compete, the Yukon Jack affair having been "a real armbuster," which he won by beating the best super-heavyweight arm wrestlers in North America (John Brzenk and Gary Goodridge, by Cleve Dean's count, who will not be in Sweden). But in arm-wrestling terms having Cleve Dean on hand is not unlike having Jack Nicklaus or Babe Ruth or Muhammad Ali on hand.

What Cleve Dean did that revolutionized arm wrestling was develop what has come to be called the top roll. When he entered the sport the basic idea was to "hook and drag"—a clockwise hooking of the (right) hand and a motion down and sideways to the pad. The top roll involves not hooking and pressing down but prorating the arm (counterclockwise) and pulling up and toward yourself. This lays open the opponent's wrist and saps his power. In the top roll you pull toward yourself, called back pressure, and toward the pad, called side pressure, and the ideal effect is a 45-degree resultant up and across and then down the table your way, with your shoulder following and adding to the power. The shoulder is actually in it from the get-go and lines up outside the pulling arm, but we are already getting beyond the basics.

Cleve Dean credits an arm wrestler named Ricky Viars with starting to develop the top roll. "But that's all he had done was start it. . . . And I just took it and developed different methods of it, different ways of gripping."

He also brought in the notion of adaptability. Most arm wrestlers, he says, "stick with what works for them seventy-five percent of the time. They don't try new things. In the hand, and the positioning alone, there could be . . . twenty-five citable variables. Now, how many variables that are uncitable would be hard for me to even tell you. I could actually watch a guy pulling and see twenty-five different changes in his style in a matter of three seconds. That's just the way the hand can go: the way the fingers are setting, the way the hand is cocked, the way the thumb is presented in the grip, where the pressure's going to be coming to or from—*whoowee.*"

These variances of position and motion and countermotion are difficult to think of and talk of discretely. "It would be hard for me to tell another arm wrestler these things. It's one big blanket. It doesn't have an end to it, it's just a round blanket, and you got to draw from it whatever you need at the time. It cain't be, 'Well, I'm gon make this move,' because in the first place you're going against people, and people can change their mind in a—in a millisecond."

If you can adapt and wield this blanket of moves in

three seconds against forces that can break your arm—most common are spiral fractures of the humerus (twist a piece of chalk until it snaps to get an idea) and avulsion fractures of the medial epicondyle (a bone-from-bone ripping off of the knob at the bottom inside of the humerus, to which all flexor muscles of the forearm attach)—you are a rare bird.

"Arm wrestling's got to be something you do instinctively; it can't be something you got to think about. If you have to think about it, it's done took too long, it's over with. It's like breathing, or opening your eyes."

A week later in airy, clean, cool-blue Stockholm, not two hundred feet from the train station, is a poster for the competition picturing Ingemar Johansson, the former world heavyweight boxing champion, and, next to him, Cleve Dean. I round a corner, and before me in a kind of plaza are about fifty blue-and-white-athletic-suited men and women. Before I can gather that these outfits suggest rather clearly that the people in them are athletes, I am distracted by a man nearby wearing lizard- or snake-skin boots and tight jeans out of which mushrooms a tight barrel chest and, out of that, tight worked-on arms—my first revelation that I have discovered arm wrestlers; he has a pinch of Skoal in his cheek and small teeth and a kind of peroxidey wide-track Mohawk hairdo—my first revelation that I have discovered Americans.

I go into the building facing this plaza thinking it a sports hall and find it to be the hotel where most of the athletes in the event (293 in all) are staying, most of them at that moment milling around in the lobby, a boggling array of twenty-seven national team uniforms, the most arresting of which are the fifty or so Japanese (twenty athletes and, I learn, thirty support troops) wearing chartreuse windbreakers with JAWA (the W in arm-wrestling logos conventionally consists of two muscled arms arm wrestling each other) logoed in red on the back and the rising sun on the left breast. Placid in the din of weigh-in, in a chair from which he has removed the seat cushions for a better fit, surrounded by a perpetual coterie of arm wrestlers who know him and don't, is Cleve Dean, asleep. Jet lag's got him. "This time's way yonder different," he says later, "than at home."

Asleep or awake, Cleve Dean will be in this lobby when he is not arm wrestling, because his room is "so small you got to go outside to change your mind!" and because sitting and talking, when they are not arm wrestling, is what most arm wrestlers really like to do at tournaments. In these gatherings, which can go into the wee hours, Cleve Dean is godlike, if a god can be invariably agreeable. He is an icon and an oracle people want to be near physically, and historically he is Big Daddy.

He will be asked to sign everything in sight by everyone in sight for the next week. He will sign hats, shirts, scrap paper, programs, notebooks; have children sit in his lap for photos; arm wrestle children for photos; have women sit in his lap for photos; arm wrestle women for photos; have men sit in his lap for photos; arm wrestle men for photos; he will sign a photograph of a man's wife and children the man has taken from his wallet. He will have black magic marker all over his hand one day, inexplicable until you see the outline of his hand traced around his signature "Cleve (Arm Breaker) Dean" on the backs of the shirts of the security guys working the event; and when his teammates suggest, "Hey, Cleve, you ought to do like the ballplayers—ten bucks a shot!" he will say, "I heard that!" and keep on signing; and when a German arm wrestler says, "Cleve Dean, you are an arm-wrestling legend! I am a fan to you!" he will say, "Thank you"; and when a fan yells, "Cleve Dean, good tournament!" he will yell back, "Good!"; and to the next hundred requests for anything he will say, "No problem"; and when an irritatingly hip British arm wrestler comes by and says in a false Southern accent, "How's it hangin', mayin?" he will say, "Oh, about so"; and when a woman on the Swedish team sits on his lap and explains why she hasn't done so before ("I vas very shy") and says, "You can come to my place?" and tells him, "Smile to the camera!" he will; and when he nods off in the bleachers and his cane slips to the floor no one will be able to tell or remember whether it is the Israelis or the Germans who get there first to hand it to him, waking him up, to whom he says, "Thank you."

Contributing to this legendary aura is Cleve Dean's walk. It is a careful, slightly stooped, stately paced, fluid-filled placing of each step, like an elephant's stepping. Sometimes he uses a cane. Sometimes it looks as if he is being careful to avoid a fall; he is like a freighter in port in the pilotage of small tugs.

As he approaches the arm-wrestling table he smiles at all

around and shakes hands with the opponent and then most
eerily seems to ignore him. He puts his elbow in the cup
(sometimes it is an actual cup, sometimes a pad from which
the elbow may not move), erects his arm, moves in close
to the table, and waits—immobile. From the rear his back
looks as tight and big as a hog's back, a particularly comfortable one you should not disturb. His face also is meaty
and frighteningly placid. It is a boyish Zen blank of con-
centration that excludes, is beyond, the person of the opponent. The opponent is in for much worse than Cleve Dean's
thinking about him. Cleve Dean is focusing on the round
blanket of citable and uncitable variables running through
his head. He is going to explode with the right variances on
the arm that he gets a handful of and gets whatever early
signals he can from. The opponent may not know about the
blanket or about the hogs in Cleve Dean's past, or about my
specious linking of him to those hogs in this moment, but he
knows he is getting a handful of an arm that has the mass of
a fire hydrant and that knows what it's doing.

The competition begins in a bizarre Americanized atmosphere—Lynyrd Skynyrd's "Sweet Home Alabama" and
Steppenwolf's "Born to Be Wild" seem to dominate the
P.A. system. A Georgian arm wrestler—the other Georgia,
which is present with a team of formidable-looking men
managed by an unformidable-looking coach reminiscent of
professional wrestling managers in the States—is wearing a
Los Angeles Raiders cap. Cleve Dean enters the left-handed
competition on the opening day, lamenting before entering

that he has not trained for left-handed pulling. It is strategic, he says, entering the left-handed competition: anyone he beats should find unfathomable the prospect of his right hand, and anyone who beats him is going to develop a false sense of security with respect to his right hand. I ask if this psychology could perhaps work against him: "Naw."

He wins this competition, easily.

Two days later he is up for the real marbles. There is a little worry in the air, but it is mostly on my part, and I don't know what's going on, so it's dismissable. But a veteran puller on the American team, Jack Sanders, is worried that Cleve's arm is too sore from the Yukon Jack tournament for good back pressure, and the Georgians are all top rolling, which requires back pressure to counter. This makes me worried again.

Cleve has been invited to sit onstage between pulls, with the referees, a privilege that would probably draw protest were it extended to anyone else. He is so large that the numerous trips from the bleachers up onto the stage and back in the course of the dozen-plus pulls necessary in a competition this large would exhaust him. No one, not even the maniacal Georgian manager, who has bloodied his head banging it into a wall over some disappointment or other by this time, makes a peep.

Before the eliminations for a class begin, all the pullers in that class are called to the stage for a lineup and to bow to the crowd, and Cleve places himself for these affairs in the middle of the line, which seems to part for and expect him there, and shakes hands as far down each side of the line as he can. Shaking hands with the competition is number three on Cleve Dean's secrets to success in arm wrestling: 1. Know the top roll. 2. Start on command. 3. Learn to read your opponent. "And by read your opponent, learn to shake hands with him, and know where he's weak at. Whether he's weak in his hand, his wrist, his arm, or where. You know." He might merely wave to a puller who doesn't look like much.

The super-heavyweight pulling begins, and, just as in boxing, interest picks up radically. People start standing up and sometimes going up to the stage and have to be called down. There have been hours of tooth-and-nail going at it: a woman has been sent to the hospital, another has collapsed in grief on losing, the Georgian manager has stormed the stage over a foul out and refused to leave it, drawing jeers and missiles. But no one has stood and crowded the stage as they do now. This is something. And it reaches its peak whenever Cleve Dean is up. The Germans and the Israelis, vying side by side to see him, have to be called down twice. The entire crowd has changed position a bit. And for the most part, in the beginning, there isn't much to see.

A pull generally lasts from half a second to half a minute, but Cleve's seem even quicker. His first opponent he drags halfway down, then he stands up a bit, pauses, and, as if doing something necessary but not particularly agreeable, presses the helpless arm down in a firm, definitive, but soft thump—or "carries him to the pad," in his gentle way of putting it. His second draw is a Hungarian, who looks to be wearing green surgical scrubs and is somehow reminiscent of Curly of the Three Stooges. A faster no-nonsense takedown, and Cleve shakes Curly's left hand while they are still in grip and raises Curly's defeated right hand. This is the courtesy extended someone who should not be at the table with him, I presume. Next it is the big Finn, whose size suggests problems, against the big other Georgian, who is the known contender. The Georgian has been beaten by John Brzenk, possibly twice, which is good news, sort of, and would be real good news if Cleve Dean's arm were not hurt. The Finn and the Georgian have their go and it is over so fast I have to ask an American arm wrestler what happened. "The Georgian top-roll him?" "I'd say he *flashed* him."

Cleve's up onstage with a guy from security rubbing onto his arm a liniment someone is hawking. His next draw is Kenny Hoban, of the wide-track Mohawk. He and Cleve have talked about their hopes that they not meet until the finals, but it hasn't worked out that way. Jack Sanders has asked Kenny what he plans to do, and Kenny has said, "Try to beat him. Have to." He goes up there to try to do that, and I, who don't know what's going on, say to Jack, "Jack, why not just concede and—"

"Really. Save his arm."

Kenny and Cleve face off at the table and we see Cleve ask him how he intends to act, and Kenny shrugs and smiles and we see his lips say "Have to" again. To this Cleve dips his face to one side almost imperceptibly and blinks his eyes slowly, respecting Kenny's doomed resolve. "Cleve's such a gentle man," Jack Sanders is saying. Cleve dumps Kenny.

Cleve comes off the stage with Kenny and says to him, "Nice fight. You hurt my arm."

Kenny says, "Thanks."

Then a huge Brazilian flashes Kenny, and Kenny pulls a Russian for fifth place and loses. Then the quarterfinals begin and Cleve flashes the big Brazilian that flashed Kenny.

Then the big Georgian flashes Cleve.

The huge hall is stunned into silence. The twenty-seven national teams, the Finns alone sounding like an entire high school basketball game; the Norwegians with their damned cowbell that someone has offered Cleve Dean money to go sit on; the ultrahip Brit, by this time drunk, going around saying "I'm going kill 'at fockin French cunt!" meaning someone (male) who has slurred him; the Georgian manager in whose path people are by this point putting crushed soda cans because he will invariably and apparently unconsciously crush them some more with his soft tennis shoes around which his slovenly pants are falling; all the people with all the Cleve Dean signature souvenirs and all the people planning to yet get theirs signed by Cleve Dean; all the Italians in their handsome blue Braccio di Ferro (Arm of Iron) suits; all the drawn-faced Russians and all the grim-faced Israelis; all the clear-faced Swedes, clean-faced Americans, and the one lone Turk—they all freeze.

There is palpable woe in the hall.

The Georgians are moving, in celebration. Their new hero, Zauri Tskadadze, at three-hundred-plus pounds and six-something and "a pretty big boy" according to Cleve Dean later, and rather gentle in aspect himself, is getting off the stage before it is not true that he just flashed Cleve (Arm

Breaker) Dean. The gymnasium has a say-it-ain't-so-Joe pall over it, as if everyone but the Georgians has just now briefly considered throwing up. But it is just briefly, because this is a double-elimination setup and Cleve Dean and the Georgian will pull again momentarily and things will right themselves then. This odd non-music of the spheres will cease.

The security man with the hot new liniment for sale with snake toxins in it goes into overdrive on Cleve's arm. He's got long hair and for a moment looks the *ur*-roadie working on a big fat rock star if the rock star could play guitar with an arm like a Smithfield ham after a roadie wobbled the meat off the bone.

Then Cleve Dean and Zauri Tskadadze are back at the table. Cleve Dean shakes the Georgian out of grip a few times, a hard sign to read. He may be deliberately tiring him or he may be honestly bothered by his grip. The Georgian looks unspooked by any of this. Someone has *trained* these sons of bitches, is the word going around. They are reported to have films of John Brzenk. It can't get much worse than this, this waiting and these not good signs, and then at GO! it gets much worse than this.

The Georgian flashes Cleve Dean *again*. The Georgians, led by their hysterical manager, explode, and beside himself and still in grip the big Georgian slams Cleve Dean to the pad again, a kind of jubilant replay. At this Cleve Dean grabs their two right hands with his left hand and slams all three to his pad, and then they scramble around in grip as if they will arm wrestle or try to again, and Jack Sanders is intoning, like a chorus, softly, "Get out of there, Cleve. Cleve, get out of there." The Georgian is smiling but Cleve Dean is not. He turns without shaking hands and quits the stage. He looks to have the cotton mouth.

The Georgians rather spill around Cleve Dean as he leaves the stage, ignoring him. He looks really only a little disturbed, but you do not want to see someone this large, with features this large, look even moderately disturbed. Everyone is quite disturbed enough. The day is rued.

I start bucking myself up already by trying to imagine all the country sayings Cleve Dean will be in possession of and will start trotting out to buck himself up with. I can't think of any, though, because for all those sayings' Bear Bryant gusto and all their invoking of our mommas and daddies and what they have told us, I don't believe in any of them, they don't work even if you can recite them, they don't work worth a damn. Cleve is hurt, I don't care what kind of there's-always-next-time-ain't-the-end-of-the-world poop is about to come out of him, if it does.

Cleve is standing behind Zauri Tskadadze and kind of whaps him in the back, shaking his head and saying as he does, "An American doesn't act that way," though Zauri can't hear him or understand him if he could, and Cleve Dean extends his hand and they shake.

Back in Pavo, Cleve Dean has butter beans and mashed potatoes and sliced tomatoes and hamburger steak and biscuits and cobbler and sweet tea at his mother's table, modest portions all. His parents have joined the Worldwide

Church of God, which proscribes pork. "After all that pork,"
he says, agreeably shaking his head.

At the bank in Pavo, Cleve Dean pulls up to the drive-in
window to deposit some logging money. "I'd like to deposit
that, please, ma'am."

"You win everywhere you went?"

"Yes, ma'am."

"What's your title?"

"World Champion again."

"Congratulations."

"Thank you, ma'am. I appreciate it."

"Have a good day."

"All right, you too."

Pulling away he says, "Why I didn't explain to 'em that I
didn't win in Sweden, it won't make any difference to them.
Only one they ever gon know about is the one in California
they see on TV anyway." A moment later: "That was a pretty
big boy. He was just solid built, he was just made. I'd love for
my right arm to have been right, and him to have to try that
all over again."

It's drizzly, and we pass swamps where Cleve Dean has
hunted ducks, and it is reminiscent of duck-hunting weather,
except it is not bone cold, and it's always bone cold for duck
hunting. I mention new technology in waders. "We didn't
use waders. We just went on in."

Apropos of nothing more than countryside sliding by,
Cleve Dean says, "I may get involved in politics."

"What?"

"May run for office soon."

"What are you going to run for?"

"I'm not even sure about that but if I told you, if I told you what I'd really like to run for, probably shock you."

"Coroner? That'd shock me."

"Naw."

"Sheriff wouldn't shock me."

"I've thought about sheriff, believe me. Actually what I'd like to run for is governor."

This makes a kind of sudden, surprising sense. Jimmy Carter was a peanut farmer who got punched in the nose by another farmer as he canvassed a mall in his bid for governor of Georgia. No one is going to punch Cleve Dean in the nose, at least not while shaking his hand.

As politics more and more becomes iconography, what icon more becomes Georgia than Cleve Dean, who with his brother shoveled corn all day out of a two-and-a-half-ton truck faster than a six-inch augur could augur it out and then played tennis half the night; who excited Don Shula without credentials; whose elder grown daughter can say of a woman he likes: "There goes Daddy's dream!" and to the question what kind of dream: "A wet dream!"; who has tobacco buyers buying him steaks; who has worked thirty-six hours straight on a tractor, meals and all; who knows hogs and says, "There's a lot of mercilessness with hogs. I get on my brother and my daddy about it. I tell 'em they just sending their souls to hell. Now, I been rough with hogs, but I don't pen 'em up and beat 'em just because they aggavating. I might hit 'em on the nose make 'em go where I want"; who, as south Georgia becomes the hottest retirement real estate in America in the next ten years, is sitting right smack dab in the middle of it, this fecund produce capital of the world, he says, with its peaches and pecans and peanuts and cotton and soybeans and corn and tobacco and tomatoes filling its fields; who is himself a large animal product of this produce; who can settle all political disputes in less than three seconds by arm wrestling; who can leave cellular phones on the seat of his open truck because people know whose truck it is while the mayor of nearby Moultrie has his car stolen and has to run down the street after it kicking it; who is the biggest redneck whether he is one or not (but who is by every sane measure a gentleman if anything at all is meant by the term today) or whether you are allowed to call him a redneck or not, who as governor will probably not only allow you to but might require you to, and you will do what he wants you to do.

In 1998, if Cleve Dean is on the gubernatorial ticket, intercept him on the campaign trail and try to shake his hand.*

---

* Cleve Dean did not run for governor. He died in 2011. In 1995, he beat Zauri Tskadadze in a rematch in Manhattan.

Hitting Back

One's personal history, it seems dangerously obvious to me, is ordered precisely as a drawer of family snapshots: it is *not* ordered, it is lost, it is illogically duplicate (there are several copies of insignificant photos, while dear ones are absent— one lives dull days again and again, while the big moments go forever underexposed), it is finally random. To recount a history, you open a drawer. You find twenty-five-year-old two-by-four-inch Smithsonian-grade black-and-whites somehow on top of last year's lousy Polaroids. You discover packets of orange negatives melted together which could yet be developed into public prints.

I think there are these orange negatives in our histories, in our heads. Take the photo of me with my harem, circa 1957. Many things are set, by this age, in that emulsion which is soon to be called one's character, and these elements and forces are readable in the photographic emulsion before us. Note my girls. Whether they have been perversely grouped like this by an adult, or whether they adore me truly, or whether I have engineered the scene myself (surely the running-board leg is my own touch), they are indubitably mine, possessed as fully as a good bigamist may

possess them on the occasion of his fifth birthday. My chief
wife is the girl at front, the tallest and the blondest, qualities
which presumably suggested to me at the time the womanly
equivalent of Forrest's fustest and mostest. She got there
first with the most by my early reckoning, and ever since, my
chief wife—filtered from the venereal welter of short grop-
ings that gets us to our longer mates—my chief wives have
been tall and they have been blond.

My leg is up on the running board: I am, in putting it
up, putting my foot *down*, taking presumptuous charge of
the situation and of all these admirers. It is the same today.

Arbitrary, foolish, with a streak of petulance and defiance, finally confident, what is implicit in this snapshot at five is extant at thirty-five.

This is a halcyon time. The nursery school in Tallahassee, Florida, where this is taken is run by a woman named Mrs. Apthorp, and her son, who is in the Army, comes home on leave and does two things which delight us: he perforates the grounds with practice foxholes, and he spreads a giant canvas tarp over an entire mimosa tree. We spend days collecting the amber, rubbery gum from now unidentifiable trees, and regard it as a kind of tribal currency (we call it goulash), poking it and handling it and bartering it in the gloom and waterproofed air beneath the living tent.

There are two shots contemporary to this one that were not taken except in the orange emulsion of my head. I will submit that they are nonetheless as telling, as durable, as this found photo. The halcyon days at Mrs. Apthorp's do not last forever (Could they? Does the scene somehow not prefigure Warren Beatty and Faye Dunaway in their doomed gangster love?), and I matriculate at kindergarten. This new school does not have the Club Med glamour and ease of Mrs. Apthorp's; we are in a meaner bourgeois affair with hired help about (at Mrs. Apthorp's you dealt with Mrs. Apthorp). One of these functionaries is a woman who works in the kitchen: that is to say, she opens and heats the #10 cans of Chef Boy-ar-dee and serves it on pastel plastic plates with compartments. She also personally attends to her nephew, a little pen-raised bastard who has not, by age four or five, learned the use of a fork. His specially large portions of Boy-ar-dee are rammed, snatched, smeared onto his pasty face with an abandon that claims half the dining area. The aunt stands protectively by, spoon and pot at the ready to reload little Gary.

At this point, I have nothing against little Gary, though I do wish he would train to fork. There he is, with the thin, gelatinous sauce of Boy-ar-dee all over him, several broken pieces of pasta plastered, annealed, to his face in the orange glue—big fat cheap soft busted spaghetti resembling maggots. And there is his aunt, moving as nimbly as can a 200- to 300-pound woman with a ten-gallon stainless pot on her hip and a large serving spoon in the air, Gary barking *More! More!* I have nothing against little Gary and his aunt.

It comes Halloween. I get up as a pirate. My mother is an accomplished costumer and does me up for years in stage-grade disguises. In the sixth grade she will get me up in drag—basic black and pearl choker, C-cup washcloth tits—and I perversely will go out *in the afternoon* for a round of solo trick-or-treating. I transfixed a man, *froze* a man, who could not close his front door as I swiveled away down his driveway, giving him a little Marilyn kiss over the shoulder. Sometime later, I heard that this fellow hanged himself in his garage, and felt the smallest tremor of complicity. There is no photo of this Natalie Wood costume, or of the pirate costume in question.

As a good pirate then, with eye-patch and short sword, I walk in on little Gary, who is on the toilet about the business of "making grunt" of his Boy-ar-dee. "Little Gary is in there making grunt," his aunt says in my fictive universe today.

Well, Gary, before I can apologize for the intrusion or even back out, runs hobbled by his pants out of the bathroom. I proceed with my business, whether making grunt or tinkling I do not recall. I manage neither operation before the mustachioed aunt crashes in, accusing me of deliberately scaring Gary, and sits me down against a wall, and commands that I remain there. I tell her the costume scared him, that I just—she will hear none of it. She leaves me there until, it seems, I am rescued by some other, higher functionary, but it is a long time I am against that wall becoming aware, for damned sure, that some people are not good people. I had no trouble filing Gary and his aunt as my very first specimens.

Now, take the photo of me, my mother, and a beagle named Gyp. We are yet in Tallahassee. An interesting thing

happens one day in this yard. There is no photo of it. That there is no photo tells more than if there were. This yard is cared for by a black man. I recall him vaguely: khaki pants, easy moves, keeping quiet. One day, upon some odd occasion that I got into a conversation with him, I did two things in the presence of my mother which represented the very cornerstones of the good manners my parents were insistent one display: I addressed the yardman as *Mr.*, and I responded to him *Yes, sir.* These are two simple but powerful tools one can use even today with startling good results, and I am fond of using them when in the presence of elders who regard the world as one of irremediable decline, and I might have been selfishly expecting some subtle profit to come from so addressing a yardman in 1957. But only moments after this exchange I was told by my mother that the *Mr.* and the *sir* were not correct. At this abrogation of absolutes I can honestly report being mystified: Why not? You just don't.

My mother put this to me gently, and, I would like to suggest, a bit sadly, for I believe we are not bigoted in any vigorous way but in the way of simple, inertial, white *status quo.* And I think the *status quo* saddle would have been an altogether comfortable one for me to ride if I had not been frightened into peeing in my pants by a three-hundred-pound mustachioed harridan protecting her fyce nephew to whom (her, not grunting Gary) I *did* have to say *Yes, ma'am.* And that same inculcated respect for elders commanded that I obey that monster and sit against that wall in a pirate suit, a respect undone for a silent, hardworking man in the sun with a worn-out, wobbly-wheeled lawn mower. Another party shot.

I am again impressed with the way these photos seem to contain, or telegraph, later character, as was suggested a bit speciously (perhaps) regarding one's lasting nursery school taste in women. In the party shot, of the same era, note the sailor-suited boy who appears particularly disapproving as the rest of us party down. He has gone on to live something of a troubled life, I hear. And I to something more like a well-adjusted partying life. There is a longer story in this picture which will yet develop the matter of respect for folk, showing it and claiming it.

Sitting on a swing, I am wearing one of my favorite suits—I will be well dressed until college, when my mother can no longer coordinate and set out my clothes so that I don't wear anything that "clashes." As, indeed, she has done here. One day, wearing this natty outfit or one like it, I had been playing with my disapproving friend, and after play,

inside, discovered *dog shit* in the pocket of this handsome
blouse. What was particularly galling was my mistaking the
matter for dirt until virtually tasting it in the course of my
assay. I concluded that my friend Don had put the shit in
my shirt: it must have slid off the hoe when he hit me in the
head with the hoe. That—being struck—was regular and ac-
ceptable. But this fouling of one's wardrobe was a bit wide of
beam, perhaps even my mother was besmirched, and I recall
this moment as my very first instant of moral outrage. I did
nothing about it.

I did nothing about it until my father did something about it, and it wasn't the shit in my pocket that motivated him, it was the screaming. My friend, as I say, was accustomed to hitting me, unprovoked, and I would repair home crying. Sometime shortly after the foul-pocket affair, I received a particularly gratuitous, open-palmed slap to the center of my back, and ran into the house wailing, a virtual emergency siren. My father grabbed me and told me I need not worry so much anymore about Don hitting me, because if he did it again, and I did not hit back, *he* would hit me. He was a belt man, and fast. I considered his promise, knew it to be genuine, and calculated that I'd be wasting time if I waited for Don to strike again. And who knew: the next blow might overwhelm me into another defenseless retreat, while I had the present affront assimilated. Emboldened by the larger fear of my father, giddy to discover it correct to clobber someone, perhaps shamed by the pure discovery that in being polite I had been apparently cowardly, and not unmindful of my nice yellow suit top with its pen pocket recently full of shit, I went to Don's house next door, stopping a moment in our carport for a tool.

I asked to see Don. Don presented himself on the screen porch, opened the door, I grabbed his arm and jerked him out, down, and across the concrete steps, and began to whale away approximately at the small of his back with a claw hammer. His mother pulled me off before I could seriously hurt him. It worked. Don never struck me again, and we spent another off-and-on ten years together.

My father told me this magical I'll-hit-you formula three

times. I am afraid it worked only this first time, if assault with a deadly weapon can be construed a workable solution (I think it can). The second time was during my first at-bat in my first Little League ball game. I was on a team of scrubs, a consolation team made up of boys too young or small or crummy to be on a competitive team (they named us the Mullets and let other teams practice on us, though as I recall only one team ever played us, rather like the Globetrotters and their dummy opponents). At the plate, I discovered I had a natural move to the bucket: you move your front or rear leg back and away from the plate, which (1) takes you out of hitting range and (2) indicates scared batter. Deep, then, in the bucket, I watched two perfect strikes zip by and was bodily lifted from the batter's box by my father. He applied the formula: "If you step in the bucket one more time, you don't have to worry about the *ball* hitting you." I knew the rest.

"It's going to hit me."

"No it's not."

"It *is*, Daddy."

"No goddammit it's *not*."

He returned to the stands. "It is," I said. I squared back in, bat held back and high (I was a superbly coached coward), watched the pitcher wind up, and closed my eyes so I could not move away, like a horse with a sack on its head in a barn fire. The ball hit me cleanly in the head with enough force to put me on the very plate, breathing clay.

"You've *killed* him, you son of a bitch!" my mother is alleged to have screamed, hitting my father. I was awarded first base and so became the only Mullet base runner all season, as I recall. I did not score. Years later, on a championship team in Jacksonville (we were the Green Turtles this time, but no scrubs, and we had the supreme pleasure of beating a team that called itself the Jets; if I were to get on a team today, it would be the Manatees or Sea Cucumbers, I'm sure), I was slugging over .600 yet was still afraid, at heart, of the ball, and today when I see Dickie Thon hit in the eye in Houston badly enough to speculatively end his career, I feel justified.

The next application of the formula was not *ad hoc* but *in genere*. If I ever got a whipping at school, I was promised a further and worse one at home. This made a pretty good boy of me. In fact, I suspect some early intimation of this public-private double whammy helped little Gary and his aunt in their rout of me, and I have even today a fear of appointed authority that might seem more appropriate in Moscow. I pay unmerited invoices. I contest no parking ticket. I am working now almost fifteen years devising a way of repairing damages for a harmless, prank theft in college. Police make me babble. I volunteer for breathalyzers lest they think ill of me.

The three shots of my father may suggest his power in the application of threatened force. From these images, and probably from my parents' collection of Elvis Presley's early 45s ("Hound Dog," "Heartbreak Hotel," "Don't Be Cruel"—these were their good years; in the sixties they graded into Perry Como and Andy Williams and Ray Conniff and His Singers), which I played relentlessly, I got

the impression that there was a closer-than-usual align-
ment between my father and Elvis. His Marine dress-blues
portrait—disappeared, but similar to the cocky portrait
here—is alleged to have been mailed home for distribution
among the girls waiting for the war to end and the fun to
begin, and the running-lizard open-field gridiron cameo
was already in the public domain. My conclusion: the old
man was fast, insouciant, competent enough to need make
no idle threat.

In the ninth grade I sat one day with a girl on a school bus
rather than, as rule stipulated, with the boys, for the simple
reason that boys were three-to-a-seat and you could sit two-
to-a-seat on the less crowded girls' side. Ahead of me another

boy sat with another girl. This was not an altogether irregular infraction, but on this particular morning the driver asked us to separate. We did not. We were summoned, the fellow ahead of me and I, to the Dean of Boys' office.

There it was alleged that we had been told by the driver to move, had done so to his satisfaction (the driver was honest in his assumption), and had then had the temerity to move back. "No, sir," I said, digging our grave a bit deeper with my ever-honest teeth. "We never moved."

"You *never moved*," the Dean said.

"No, sir," we both said.

"What if there'd been a fire on the bus and the driver told you to move?"

"That's different," one of us must have essayed. (I recall *fire* being involved in curious relation also to long hair and leaning back in desks during these enlightened years. How anyone survived public education where I took it I do not know.)

We explained that the segregated-sex rule made no sense to us because of the crowding on the male half of the bus, that girls were often sitting alone. Our interrogator, I'll call him McDaniel, here turned in his oak swivel chair and stared out the window for a full three minutes, leaving us standing in front of his desk. During his study of the outdoors, he sighed heavily and rubbed his stubble. At last he swung around.

"Boys, do you know *why* we have this rule?"

That was precisely it! We couldn't begin to know. "No, sir."

"Well, I'll tell you." More face-rubbing—his beard, at ten

thirty, was as heavy as card teeth for cleaning files. "This year you know we are *integrated*."

"Yes, sir," one of us must have said, allowing the other to work on this surprising tack.

"Well, how would you feel," the Dean said to Greg (Greg Nystrom, whose real name I'll use on pain of suit to correctly honor the small heroism he was about to effect), "how would you feel if one of them *sat with your sister?*"

(I realize this tableau is perhaps incredibly close to the hackneyed *marrying* of one's sister, but you may as well believe this went down as depicted—I could render it less trying to credulity by adjusting some fictional stops.)

(One other thing: it had come out in prior testimony that *I* was sitting with Greg's sister, a fact we naively submitted in the hope that the crime of sitting with girls would somehow be mitigated by the sister-brother complicity, as though in fact we might have all just been on some kind of cozy, non-sexual double date.)

To the Dean's question, Greg Nystrom said, "I wouldn't mind, if he was a nice guy."

"I didn't *ast* you what kind of GUY he was! How would you *feel?*" The Dean of Boys was right worked up. We were oddly calmed by his seething—relieved to discover, I suppose, a larger issue in all of this than our simple disobedience.

Calmly, Greg started again: "Well, if he was a nice guy and all—"

"I don't care what kind of guy he is!" the Dean shouts.

I am at this point a virtual spectator, in a kind of intellectually and sexually rapt state: *It was me*, I'm thinking,

I'm the guy. I am horny enough at this age to do sufficient harm, you may be sure, and perhaps I'm amused at this, but to state I was lost in complex and moral speculations is not correct. I was taking, simply, an odd pleasure standing on these junior-high gallows for my imaginary foil, thinking it would be nice to . . . whatever with Greg's sister, thinking maybe I wasn't *nearly* so nice as our imaginary demon, and enjoying my accidental subbing for him.

Meanwhile, the Dean is steaming, nostrils burning, when Greg says, "I wouldn't care."

"You wouldn't care."

"No, sir."

"How about you?" the Dean says to me.

"*I* wouldn't care. *I* was the one sitting—"

"God *damn!* That's not the point!"

We stood there, waiting for the point. Here it came.

"You can take swats or bus suspension."

I asked how many swats versus how many days off the bus, and the Dean asks me if there's something *wrong* with me, and I say no, I'd just like to know (I am calculating the odds also of keeping this whole affair quiet at home—it will be remembered that the duplicate whipping will presumably be in effect). It comes out to three swats or three weeks, and that's too long to ride a bike ten miles, so we get our asses blasted smartly three times with a polished one-by-two wielded by a state-funded, certified, pensioned redneck.

I go home and keep all of this a secret, and don't know what might have happened had I revealed it. I suspect the I'll-hit-you double jeopardy or some perverse latter-day expression of it would have obtained, but I like also to think I might have gotten the bastard fired. Of all one's dumb days, of all the stupid things one has said and done and keeps saying and doing, of all one's small retreats from honor, this is one event I would yet like to play differently. I would like to get a hammer and go back and repay the Dean. I wish I had said to him that I'd accept neither punishment until I called the NAACP and both our parents, for starters, and my family's lawyer, and seen what might have happened.

And I do not feel so hot today for the very suspicion that one is yet being told by brutes to sit against the wall while the non-meek inherit the earth, to not sit with the girls for reasons you'd never guess. One gets the large feeling of returning home most days without hitting back. That little nausea is at the root, perhaps, of deciding to write—deciding at last, however feebly, to defend oneself, to hit back.

The Pacific WWII scenes combined in my mind with the running lizard and the Presley sneer to create an image of carefully successful violence on demand, an instantaneous access to violence so successful, upon demand, in fact, that its threat your way would motivate a child to hammer another in the sacral plate, take a beanball with grace, conceal the graceless hazing of juveniles by a grown bigot. It is, though, this violence, an inviable thing to me, a thing which, if I had, I could . . . relax. The connection may be specious, but look (in the Pacific shots) how relaxed these guys are! It looks like a movie set—my father could be Martin Sheen filming *Apocalypse Now* in the Philippines. One sees no photographs

of Vietnam that suggest this quality of comfort within war. Yet this was war. Things were nasty enough that my father deliberately tells no war stories other than these: (1) The Japanese were tougher than we were, and unjustly provoked into fighting by our limiting their efforts at peaceful expansion (I have always found this a generous sentiment to come from an All-Southern halfback who claims this fighting "walked his legs off"—to an unresilient and unplayable condition upon his return at the seeming prime of twenty-four). And (2) a tale of a typhoon that hit and kept hitting for three days, driving rain so hard it cut flesh, ripping tents which were tied to a cable strung between two earth graders, and even the earth graders were moved! After the blow, they emerge from the shredded canvas heaps, and "Yankees" who have never seen hurricanes, he says, are "white as sheets" for another three days. Then they get back to the business at hand, and though the Japanese *soldiers* might be a little more bulldoggy than ours, our scientists appear a little quicker than theirs, and so a lot more of these relaxed Martin Sheens than might have come home *do* come home, and with these "preternatural tans" (just read this somewhere) claim wives away from the high school boys and put on the ground the next wave of Pacific soldiers and record their childhoods in these snappy little Eastman Kodak works of art. At any rate, though, we struck back.

The remaining pictures sustain or impel one toward the odd resolution to strike back on paper. The first rather obviously: evolving from her very book is my maternal grandmother,

whose five novels, one dedicated to me and read at an early age (so early that I wasn't sure I wasn't *in* the book), and whose estranged life in New York lent hope of one's own eventual writerly big time (I have always preferred to believe, though, that the publication party pictured here was not in New York but in Port St. Joe, Florida, where the novel is set).

What you need, when you begin to dabble with the fool notion that you can somehow take a hammer to the world with paper and print, is good, solid convincing that you are nut enough to support the notion long enough to strike. My pistoling, noveling grandmother is here seen posing not with an uncle of mine, as I thought for years, but with her new husband (he is both the gangster and the football player). She has spurned, it would seem, my real grandfather, seen here (with my mother) gaunt and stern, an accomplished scrubland jack-of-all-trades (house painting to school principaling) whose salient characteristic seems in the long view to have been bad luck with his women (his third wife, no picture, is believed by at least three surviving members of our shrinking clan to have poisoned him—twice). He is unique among us also for his temperate stand against alcohol, one he took after winding up in jail *both* times in his life he drank. The rest of us are openly practicing clinical cases of one description or another.

Here, in fact, balding, is my other grandfather, about whom I know only that he was "a hair-jerker" (my father's phrase, and indicative, one may presume, of the somewhat milder I'll-hit-you disposition), and that he was a beverage agent in a dry county who successfully used the job

to protect Alachua County bootleggers. And my paternal grandmother (of the cross-legged women, she's on the left): in my long, undetailed view, she was an avid poker player who belted jiggers and shuffled cards with the same rapid motions of a person washing her hands.

The authorities for whom my grandfather worked popped in one day with a bit of a plan. They put my grandmother in the back seat, had my grandfather drive, and went to a known bootlegger's where my grandfather was to ask for whiskey himself—a ploy designed to prove he was in cahoots not merely at the level of graft but, as it were, up to his gills. Presumably the total want of arrests in his county had raised a brow or two.

At the bootlegger's, my grandfather placed the order (of a family friend, to boot), and from the back seat, where she had been put to prevent her phoning ahead, my grandmother called ahead anyway with a "high sign," as family legend puts it—what specifically she did that warned a man outside the car, without signaling those inside the car, I don't know, but I suspect it came from the theater of poker.

Once, forty years later, she escaped from a nursing home as I arrived to visit. The staff was indeed hair-tearing, frantic, for she was frail and it was hot and she was gone. Apparently inserting the family template for escape, I walked directly across the most dangerous thoroughfare adjacent the home, into the absolute densest apartment complex in sight, and then directly to the small entrance foyer where she had given out, pink-gowned and blinking in the sun. "What *took* you so long!" she said to me in a high, dramatic overdrawl that would have been the envy of all the bad actresses who have ever played Blanche DuBois, and she was baffled that I did not, according to our imaginary conspiracy, provide the means necessary to effect her complete getaway.

The pictures of my mother should speak of a theatricality undiluted, and the one of my brothers of white mice,

their hair kept short during these Goldwater-all-the-way days for experimental purposes. And here I hold one of the free world's last indigo snakes (I mean, we needed no state permit to possess this now on-the-brink fellow)—drawn to snakes early, I was, because by my lights they truly can find no real way of hitting back, and I am here prepared to defend them with the zeal of a carnival barker.

My conclusion: there is photographic evidence of enough nut blood and thespian gameness in this my clan to get any but the truly uninterested off to a well-grounded start in the art of assembling strange truths into less strange lies—to a soaring faith in the improbable belief that with pen and paper one can hit back.

Juan Perez

On October 8, 2012, Mr. Juan Perez, drummer for the Beth McKee Band, drove from his house in Orlando over to the Orange Blossom Trail and through the vestigial orange grove surrounding the old ranch-style house that serves as the Randall knife factory and went in and picked up, for $372.75, his Denmark Special, in O1 tool steel, a knife he has wanted for fifty years since running around Orlando hunting small game with boys better off than he who had Randalls, one of the boys in fact a friend of Pete Denmark for whose father's store the knife is named, that's complicated, let's move on. Mr. Juan Perez did not have to wait the current fifty-three months to have his Randall made.

On November 9, 2012, Mr. Juan Perez got in the band van with his new Randall rolled up in a face towel with its sheath (but not *in* its sheath, *acid in that leather*) and drove to Tallahassee to play a gig later that night at the Bradfordville Blues Club, a historically black club enjoying three distinctions: that it is still operating, that it is on the Mississippi Blues Trail, a fancy historical marker attesting to that effect in front of the club under the live oak known as the dog tree because "all the dogs" are said to be buried under the tree, the category of dogs constituting "all the dogs" unknown, and that it is on the Mississippi Blues Trail without being in Mississippi. The drive was long, and one of the members of the band said he'd like to see a porno made of Mayberry, and the band agreed that Helen Crump was very hot, and someone said it would be good if Barney Fife, played by Don Knotts, had a huge member, and Mr. Juan Perez said, "In fact he did. It was so big his friends called him Dong Knotts."

In the ranch-style house that serves as the band house for the visiting bands that play the Bradfordville Blues Club it was perceived that there was no proper bedroom for the bassist, Mr. Dan Walters, and to prevent his having to sleep on a hide-a-bed with that troubling bar Ms. Melissa King, who accompanies the guitarist Joe King and who recently told Paul Thorne that she overheard two women in the restroom before his show saying that they felt he, Paul Thorne, was a panty melter, dragged the top half of her and Joe's bed into the den and made it up on the floor for Mr. Dan Walters. Paul Thorne took the stage and announced that he had just been told by a nice lady that she'd heard women in the restroom calling him a panty melter and that he had never heard of that but supposed it was a good thing.

The band talked a long time before the show and after the show, which was not well attended, which bummed the band out, which made the after-show talk last until three a.m. without drugs or alcohol, and Mr. Juan Perez said, "The first time I saw the Allman Brothers live, I just stood there not quite understanding what I was listening to. *What is going on?* I got as close as I could to the side of the stage and lined up Jaimoe and Butch Trucks. They were playing different patterns but when it came to the fill, they were instantly synchronized. I'd never seen anything like that before," and he also gave his impression of Dick Morris, rolling his eyes in a comical manner reminiscent of the grandfather clock on *Captain Kangaroo* and attempting to have spittle fly out of his mouth, "I am the Truman Capote of Republican strategith, if it hadn't been for Thuperthorm Thandy thealing Mither Romneeth momentum, I believe he would have eathily won the electhion," and of his prostate surgery he said, glass half fully, "I was continent in four months." Then the band went to bed.

In the morning the band drove out Centerville Road to Bradley's Country Store to get mostly sausage. They proved far from alone in deciding to go to Bradley's to get sausage on a Saturday morning and there were at times maybe fifteen people in line in front of the meat counter so the band sat down at a small table that had a display of Case knives in it and Mr. Juan Perez, at this point wearing his Randall in its sheath on his belt, took it out and put it on the glass over the lesser knives and they took a photograph of it. They sat there in the agreeable country kitsch of the place, mule collar on the wall, Mullet salt and fresh 5

cents the pound from Wakulla Springs on the wall, a band
member showed Beth McKee a roll of kerosene-lamp wick
for sale and she did not know what it was so he told her it
was lamp wick, and then they caught a lull in the line and
bought 7 lb. mild smoked sausage, 2 lb. hot smoked sausage,
2 lb. mild fresh sausage, 1 lb. hot fresh sausage, 1 Coke, 1
Barqs, 1 six-inch mild fresh sausage dog w/ mustard, onions & relish, 1 six-inch mild fresh sausage dog w/ mustard,
sauteed onions and peppers & coleslaw, 1 twelve-inch hot
smoked sausage dog w/ mustard, onions & coleslaw, 1 large
bag Tostitos scoops, 1 jar black bean & corn salsa made especially for Bradley's, 1 bottle Aquafina water, and 1 bag
Lays (because certain sandwiches require traditional po-
tato chips), and Mr. Juan Perez took out his Denmark Special and pressed it exactly at the halfway point deliberately
and calmly through the twelve-inch hot smoked sausage
dog w/ mustard, onions & coleslaw, stopping without cutting the paper beneath the sandwich. Then he wiped and
sheathed the blade.

The band went outside and loaded their purchases into
the van and noticed a man getting out of a truck near the
smokehouse and a band member asked him, "Are you con-
nected to this operation?" and he said at one time he was
but he was now retired, he was Frank Bradley, and Frank
Bradley showed them the sausage-making room, and the
federal inspector's office, telling them that at one time they
had a lot of trouble with the Florida meat inspectors until all the local sausage people militated to get rid of the

Florida meat-inspection program and with the help of
Senator George Kirkpatrick they did, and he showed them
where the hogs come in and are stunned and bled and the
scalding trough (148 degrees) and the big swaged lever to
flip the hog, they like about a 240-pound hog, into the
tumbler that whaps most of the hair off the hog, of which
there can be eighteen to twenty in a normal week and as
many as fifty a week in the holidays, so many that they have
to go to Liberty County or even Tennessee to get enough
hogs, and a 240-pound hog makes 125 pounds of sausage
you do the math, and he showed them the smokehouse
which was hard to see the sausage in because of the smoke,
and the external firebox which was essential in not starting
the fires in the smokehouse they had to contend with when
the firebox was internal in the old days, and the hickory
corded up by the box, and he showed them the grist mill in
the nicely restored mill house with the fifty empty bags of
corn ground yesterday still beside the grinder, and he told
them Bradley's grits can be eaten with a fork and others
have to be eaten with a spoon, and he told them he was
having knee surgery Monday and he trusted his doctor because he had already had him do three hip replacements, he
is eighty-seven, his grandmother started Bradley's in 1910
selling sausage out of her kitchen window, it is still her recipe they use, people seem to like it, what worries him is the
knee giving out going down stairs and his falling, his father
in the beginning delivered sausage to Tallahassee, to stores,
banks, you name it, but at a point he said, If you want this

sausage you can come get it and stopped delivering it, and he, Frank Bradley, took over the business in 1963 and now his daughter Janet has it, and we stood there in the crisp fall north-Florida air redolent of smoked meat, and I suppose there might have been a better place to be at that moment, you could be, say, having you a brandy at Le Grand Colbert brasserie in Paris on a Saturday morning watching cultivation go by, people who like to say the United States is racist but who themselves have yet to elect a black man to head up their free democratic operation, come to think of it the United States is the only white-majority country to have elected a black man its leader, or you could be just there in the sand yard at Bradley's talking to Mr. Bradley, hoping his surgery goes okay, doing fine.

Then the band continued out Centerville Road until it becomes Mocassin Gap Road and eventually leads more or less right to Reeves Landing Campground and Fish Camp on Lake Miccosukee, the lake so low in preparation for burning the vegetation in it that if it weren't for some good beer drinkers Eli Reeves would not be able to hang on, and then the band drove to Capps, Florida, and stopped at the historic home of Mr. Robert Olen Butler, who had one wife run off with his two parrots and another wife run off with Ted Turner, but Mr. Robert Olen Butler was not there, he was at NoirCon where he was the keynote speaker, and his new wife, also the new mayor of Capps, showed them two of the perfectly appointed rooms in the historic house and gave them Mr. Butler's new book and they went on back to Orlando, whence Beth McKee reported, "The minute we hit the door last night, [Mr. Juan Perez] had the WD-40 and some other polishing product out on the kitchen counter cleaning the sausage grease and mustard off the Denmark. Heh heh."

C. Ford Riley

I agreed to profile a painter named C. Ford Riley in Jacksonville, Florida, because I am from Jacksonville, Florida, too and I thought perhaps we could develop some happy harmonies owing to our common background which, the happy harmonies of common background, would help mask my ignorance of painting and painters. Perhaps the schools C. Ford Riley went to would not be distant from the schools I went to etc. Perhaps some striking mutual accordance would allow me to not talk about painting and painters altogether, and I could ride a cavalry of distraction around my weak knowledge and obscure it altogether. When I called C. Ford Riley and asked where he went to high school he said Lee and I said my mother taught at Lee and he said "You sound like a local boy" and I said "I went to Lake Shore Junior High" and he said "*I* went to Lake Shore" and I said I heard Allen Collins play a guitar when we were fourteen years old in the cafeteria and was transfixed by how good he was because all I had ever known Allen to do was walk the halls dreamily when he was not suspended, and C. Ford Riley said one day when he and Allen were suspended for sniffing glue he and Allen went to his house in

Ortega and practiced their guitars in the garage and later they decided to practice as a band there and his mother, he said, took one look at Bob Burns, the original drummer for the band this would become, and said, "You will not be doing this," or words to that effect, so C. Ford Riley formed another band, called the Chain Gang, which did nothing, and Allen and Bob were in a band called the One Percent, which I followed for three years as ardently as a band can be followed by a groupie, female or male, and C. Ford Riley went on to teach himself how to paint and Allen and Bob became rock stars. Then Bob quit the band, I thought, or they kicked him out, C. Ford Riley thought, but either way he was not on the plane when Lynyrd Skynyrd crashed, to die as Ronnie Van Zant did, or to survive and die later as Allen did.

I told C. Ford Riley that I read that Bob Burns was once talked into quitting the band by a girlfriend who found it appalling that he would be having to eat a fish that he caught after being in that band for so long and I wondered if the girlfriend who persuaded him into this boneheadedness was the lovely Ann Allen, who had been his girlfriend at Lake Shore. C. Ford Riley did not know Ann Allen and I did not expect him to because despite her civility she seemed to have come from the other side of the tracks from Ortega, but she had had a somewhat more genteel-seeming friend named Sue Scherer who maybe was from Ortega, and C. Ford Riley said, "I know Sue Scherer well." It felt to me that the cavalry of distraction I wanted to run around the weak army of my main mission was very well placed and active and dependable. If I went up to Jacksonville and had my ignorance exposed in the studio I could suggest we call Bob Burns and Ann Allen and Sue Scherer and have a party.

The painters I know personally are Kathy and Jim Muehlemann of Blacksburg, Virginia; my college roommate James Pritchard of New York City when I last saw him; a fellow in New Orleans named Aaron Collier who has painted a buffalo with a human nose on it that he has offered to me; Dan Lomahafteewa, a Hopi Indian from whom I bought a painting of a Hopi deity; David Deutsch, a friend of William Wegman; and William Wegman. Of these I know William Wegman the best and I called him to ask him if he knows of C. Ford Riley and he was not there but his wife, Christine Burgin, an art dealer, was.

"Christine, are you still thin?"

"In certain places."

"You know that kind of painting that features marshes and ducks and is popular at craft fairs? What is that called if it is not to be called realistic or wildlife art or if the painter does not want it called realistic or wildlife art?"

"Well, if it is the kind that hangs in English mansions it can be called Sporting Art. Realism is generally better than realistic." (This makes sense: we know to never say simplistic, but we can say simple if we are careful.)

"How are the dogs?"

"They are fine."

"Who are the dogs now?"

"Candy, and Bobbin, and Penny."

Bill Wegman keeps a crew of Weimaraners on hand

to work with and is so well known for his work with them that some people do not know he is a painter. I have heard a painter in fact resent the kind of money he can make for a painting and have reported this to Bill, who has said, "Tell him I have paid my dues." I have watched Bill play with a canvas and make things appear out of nowhere and have been amazed at the deftness with which he can do this and at what I would call the purity of line if it did not sound so fey.

I did not know the dog Man Ray, who began Bill's career as a famous dog artist, but I knew Fay (Ray) and Batty and Chip and Chundo, and now I know Candy and Bobbin (Ray) and Penny. The dogs go everywhere that Bill goes.

C. Ford Riley has a dachshund named Gator who recently suddenly went stone deaf, so it is possible to sneak into the house without his knowing you are in it and without your having to take him with you when you leave it. The studio, detached from the house, overlooking live-oak hammock and a ravine going down to the St. John's River, a majestic thing up to three miles wide at this point, is a power studio. There are four guitars upright in front of four Peavey amps, six small paintings over the fireplace mantel (one of them a simple, strong study of a blue jay), a fireplace blocked by a painting of saltwater marsh, two light easels supporting small paintings in corners, a large Turkish kilim on the floor covered with deformed tubes of oil paint and paper towels and Q-tips and foam plates employed as palettes (at the end of work these plates are capped with a clean plate and stacked), five or six or seven or nine or seventeen other paintings leaned upright here and there, Solo cups half-filled with paint water, one hopes, a Beatles CD, and a gilt-framed mirror on the floor facing a large central easel, which is a Hughes 4000 of heavy and finely crafted oak suggesting cathedral furniture or artillery carriage or a medieval siege appliance or part of a ship. "That," C. Ford Riley says, "is the best easel in the world. It will go to the ceiling."

Of the mirror on the floor facing the easel, C. Ford Riley says, "I work through a mirror. That's how I paint. If you look at it through there"—looking not at the painting on the easel but at the painting in the mirror—"you can see where it's going to go, for the most part."

He demonstrates. To work on a painting, C. Ford Riley puts it in a real frame of the sort likely to hold it in real life— say a heavy gilt frame—and sits to the right of the canvas about two feet from it. At this working distance, looking at the mirror about eight feet away reflecting the painting adds about fourteen feet of light distance between the viewer and the painting; it simulates looking at the painting across a goodly sized room. The sudden vantage from being on top of the painting to seeing it as if across the billiards parlor or the main room of the lodge is a jolt, as if a visual trick is at hand. The long view conveys a sudden power and exactitude and correctness one does not see close up.

On the Hughes 4000 is a painting of a sand-bottomed blackwater creek in southeastern river bottom. It is . . . perfect. It is the kind of image that makes you want to be there, now, or to say that you have been there, many times, or to own the creek, or to say that you own the creek—or all of the above. If you are the kind of person susceptible to this odd rush of emotions, it is also the kind of image that will make you want to buy the image. And if you *do* actually own the creek, as some people do, you will *have* to buy the image. This phenomenon, this compulsion to claim kinship with or possession of the scene in this kind of painting when it is *correct*, I surmise—knowing nothing of which I speak, picking up a small knife that I do know something about—is the keystone to C. Ford Riley's success. His audience will prove to be the set of people subject to this weird land fever and the subset of people who do own the land.

The knife I have picked up has paint on it that would suggest it is used for apportioning paint by cutting extruded lines of it from the tube and is a Randall knock-off made by a defunct outfit called Black Jack out of Effingham, Illinois, and C. Ford Riley says, "Are you familiar with Randall knives?" and I tell him I am, and he says, "I'll tell you one thing, this is a sharp-ass damn knife and I have never sharpened this knife and it's still—well, you see what *I* use it for. But I've got a Randall knife. It's this big. My father-in-law gave it to me—twenty years ago." He shrugs. "And I knew of Randall knives. Well, this is great but then I'm thinking, What the hell did you buy this for? I mean what do you *use* it for? It's too small for a machete"—he makes a slashing X in the air—"too big for . . ."

"Meat."

"*Anything.*"

A Randall knife is a perfect symbol at the center of this passion for land and hunting on land and it is the knife for the purest enthusiasts of this sort in the United States. The knives, made in Orlando, Florida, had their formative moments in Michigan with roundabout connections to Hemingway and a circle of hunting men.

Speaking of the river-bottom painting, C. Ford Riley says, "This is on some property over in Thomasville, Georgia. I love it over there. I just love river bottom. And this is all river bottom and this is actually fall . . . well it would be in another month from now, month, month and a half. And things are losing their leaves but you still have some greenery and you still have some stuff in there. This is actually a place called Hadley Creek, which runs into the Ochlocknee."

A Valuable Aside Concerning Hadley Creek, or Near It, from the Late Boatbuilder Robb White of Thomasville, Georgia

"Another thing about Robert . . . he was in the train wreck when the shaky trestle over the Ochlocknee River at Hadley Ferry broke down and the sawmill train fell in the river and scalded all those men to death in 1925. He was the fireman in the engine and ought to have been the first one to die but he dove under the water and, though the concussion of the implosion made him bleed out the ears, he was the only survivor of the whole crew . . . had to walk twenty miles to tell the news and nobody believed him because he was just a (. .) (I ain't going to say that word because my Momma taught me not to)." [Robb White website, Grumman Sport Boat]

I ask C. Ford Riley if the worst thing he can be called is a wildlife artist. I do not know precisely how I have divined this might be a sore spot, but I have.

"I started painting birds, you know, thirty years ago, studying birds, I mean I studied birds and I painted them for my own benefit, just for my own studies, and then you know it evolved that people started buying my studies and the next thing I knew, Hey, I can, I can make a living doing this, pay for my beer and do whatever. Your typical twenty-year-old mentality.

"And then I evolved into painting the *habitats*, which I *love* to paint. And from there I've just evolved into just so many different other facets.

"The term 'wildlife art.' When I see people that paint lions and tigers and they live in Colquitt, Georgia"—he shakes his head—"you know, well, I guess that's fine with me, it's just, I don't know how people . . . with me I've just got to paint what I know and what I can feel, or I can smell or, you know, eat or whatever.

"I've got nothing against it, there're some great artists out there that, that do very well, you know, but I'm more . . . the art that I like has come down through the Old Masters."

C. Ford Riley mentions the German Hermann Herzog who lived and painted in Florida and whom he calls another "habitat" painter, Willard Metcalf ("He's an impressionist. I love all the American impressionists more than I do the French impressionists because I can relate to it—I like the color scheme more"), Winslow Homer, Edward Hopper ("I *love* Edward Hopper's work"), Frederic

Church, John Frederick Kensett, William Trost Richards, the Ruskin movement, William Merritt Chase, Childe Hassam. If a layman glances at the work of a number of the painters on this list, he sees a style in use called luminism, which is apparently defined as a set of techniques that heighten the effects of light, and make it an element in the painting itself, for romantic purpose. He sees also painting that he would have called impressionistic if not instructed otherwise.

"I like the Ruskin movement. You have to portray nature in the sense that it's got to be *right*. You don't just put trees in the landscape for the sake of there being trees. You've got to know that they're part of that habitat. You've got to be true to nature."

"Does the epithet *realist* or the adjective *realistic* bother you, or is it agreeable, and how inaccurate is it?"

"Well, photorealism is something I don't care for at all. Not one bit at all. To portray something that... I don't know how to say it: if I can convey... if someone looks at this painting and goes, if they can go, 'I know exactly where that is or I've been there.'"

"There are distortions in this that make it more real than real?"

"I would say so. Because if you look close. You know, you go, Well, this area, I can't really tell what this *is*, but if you look *there*"—in the mirror—"then you can."

"How does this work when you say you use the mirror?"

"Well, because I just always have, you know? I just, it's something I just picked up thirty years ago. I notice stuff through a mirror and it's easier to see stuff through a mirror. And I paint for this distance anyway. And people can come up—it's almost like playing, like you say, a broken chord on a piano. It's more interesting to play a broken chord than it is just a straight-out chord. So I want to convey that realistic *sense* . . ."

"Is the mirror just a quick way of getting distance or is it doing something else?"

"I can see *passages* through this, you know, I can see like this whole thing back here, and I can pull all this up. And then I can, you know I work, it's easier for me to get my harmonies, my values, and edges when I do this."

Clearly the mirror is doing something else besides getting distance: I have not said anything about playing a piano, broken chord or straight (if I know less about something than painting, it is music). I take this broken-chord business to be a fair stab at the impressionistic heart in C. Ford Riley: he wants a broken reality to convey a realistic *sense*.

There is a large painting leaning nearby that looks to me like the backside of Cumberland Island, looking north from about Plum Orchard with the Crooked River coming in from the upper left (northwest) of the painting, and I say, "This looks like the backside of Cumberland Island, that's the Crooked River coming in there, this is about Brick Hill or Plum Orchard—"

"That's *exactly* where this is! How'd you know?"

"I know exactly where that is *and* I've been there."

"But this is at about Greystone."

"Greystone? You mean Greyfield?"

C. Ford Riley does mean Greyfield, Greyfield Inn, on Cumberland, where I imagine he stayed to do this work. The last time I checked, prices at Greyfield—one of the bivouac points for the Kennedy wedding—were $275. When I am on Cumberland I go for the $4 back-country permits, having been already wounded deeply by the $17 ferry fare. C. Ford Riley's Cumberland painting before us is also perfect, and notable in it, in the overlookable foreground, is some shallow water that is slightly disturbed exactly as it would be disturbed were mullet just below its surface. This, not the exactitude of the scene that allows one to recognize the backside of Cumberland Island looking north, is what is amazing. There is a reason that C. Ford Riley has said Greystone when he has meant Greyfield.

At the end of his sophomore year in college, which was Shorter College in Rome, Georgia, a school he selected because he had met a girl he got on with who went there (a boy in Ortega out of Lee High School might have been expected to go to, say, Washington & Lee or Duke), C. Ford Riley pushed a Coke machine off the sixth-story balcony of the Greystone Building in downtown Rome. (The building was being used as a men's dormitory; from the Shorter College website: "A significant innovation in the history of the college came in the early 1950s when school administrators and trustees made the decision to recruit the first male students. The 'Girl's Creed' had to be abandoned, a dormitory for men constructed, new sports teams created, fraternities initiated,

and very different rules of conduct established.") The Coke
machine produced, he says, a very gratifying explosion in the
street below. He was "politely asked" not to return to school
until he had gone through "some bullshit"—fairly, he says,
because even though he had "a crew of guys to help me, it was
my idea, and I *was* the one last seen touching it."

He and his friends got jobs bartending that summer at
Annie Tique's, the first flashy restaurant to arrive in Jacksonville Beach, and sold pot to Navy guys, and C. Ford Riley
started selling his bird studies also for up to $200 apiece,
which he says at the time was good money. The police scared
them out of selling dope, which he says at the time was a
good thing, and at the end of the summer even without the
lucrative drug trade they had good jobs and saw no reason to
go back to school.

And C. Ford Riley began to realize he could make a
living painting birds. His mother painted and had told
him, while dying relatively young of cancer, that he should
concentrate on what he really wanted to do, and he had
told her—"a pact with my mother"—that he would be the
best he could be in his field. She set him up with some les-
sons with the local bird painter Fred Wetzel, who Riley
says was good enough to "let me develop my own style."
In Riley's memory there was not more than a day together
in what might be called formal instruction. "What I have
done with my work and my approach is I have looked at
what the best was—in any field. I have picked it apart and
studied it and set a standard—how do I beat that standard?
Like the Beatles, for example. They never stopped in the

same format. They had an unbelievable way of changing things."

"Today, the art today, you wouldn't believe the number of people that don't know how to draw. They flash a slide up onto a canvas or whatever it might be, and then they trace out and they paint and try to copy exactly what they've got there. And like it's been said—I don't know whether I read it or heard it, or something, but it just says it perfect: That kind of, when a person works like that it's like throwing a microwaveable dish and, and then calling yourself a chef. A great chef. And that"—a backhanded wave of disdain—"you can spot right off the bat. In all genres too. It's not just this, it's everything."

We put a painting of three turkeys on the big easel and frame it with the big gilt frame. The turkeys are themselves framed by two old longleaf pines. Thus they are recognizable as Thomasville turkeys. Thomasville is itself recognized as the epicenter of the last real original forest in the southeast United States, the last stand of the longleaf pines and wiregrass that is said to have extended from Virginia to Florida to Mississippi in one monolithic unbroken park-like terrain that allowed a man to see a deer a half mile away in the woods. The connoisseur of *land* east of the Mississippi regards these hundred-foot three-hundred-year-old trees towering over their one-foot-high carpet of burnable grass as the best land there is. Other land is sometimes called "second growth and snakes," its trees a mixed bag of hardwoods and lesser pines and deciduousity and vines and other crap that is, really, just *weeds*.

C. Ford Riley realizes that I might not be altogether aboard in comprehending pulling this up and pushing that back, getting harmonies and values and edges, broken chords and straight-out chords, either through the mirror or without the mirror, and says, "Well, I can show you. Let's see if I can fuck this up right in front of your eyes," and I say, "That'd be great," and we regard the turkeys, standing at the center of this painting with a wary eye to the viewer and, to my eye, ready to run. C. Ford Riley interprets the mental state of the middle turkey: "Gentlemen, we better get the fuck out of here because I know something is about ready to happen." ("My favorite thing to hunt is turkey, but what I really like is to call them, just fuck with them.") And indeed the middle turkey does seem to be in a slightly more advanced state of alert than the others, and seems to be in charge. It strikes me that it might not be easy to depict shades of mental acuity in turkeys standing in the woods. It might not be easy to *perceive* shades of mental acuity in turkeys standing in the woods. That might require some thought and some experience on top of a good hand with the paint.

The majestic longleaf pines framing the turkeys, and the turkeys themselves, seem finished in a way that the area behind the turkeys is not—a bayhead or a descent to a river bottom, an area altogether more messy than the clean pines and birds at the front. It is this area C. Ford Riley wants to work. He daubs in some very dark brown oil in a vertical column that would have to be a tree but that looks as he does it like certifiable fucking up.

"I want it to go really far back, so I'm pulling all this up."

He makes some frightening casual sideways wavelike strokes with an alarmingly large (two-inch) regular house-painting brush to the left of the new improbable brown-tree mess, making more mess to its left in paint that was already there. "I know what I had underneath that, so without doing too much"—he takes now a tool that looks like a sharp eraser on a brush handle—"I can take, take and create more ideas here." The eraser is scribbling and doodling through the dragged two-inch-brush chaos and the new dark-brown-tree improbability leaving trails of apparently no paint at all, lines of almost clean canvas, that look like grapevines in the air or a lightning strike on the bark of the new tree or like, really, nothing at all except more mess and certifiable fucking up, except that already things look more real than they did a minute ago before they got so messed up. The new tree suddenly looks exactly as if it might have been killed by lightning with those weird rips in the bark spiraling down the trunk. "And then," C. Ford Riley says, picking up a paper towel and wadding it, "I'll go back"—mashing the wad of towel into the new brush-and-eraser scribbling—"and then I'll go back generally and I'll look at that and go either, Okay, this will work, or, That won't work"—vigorous mopping and pressing and rolling and wiping with the towel—"but most of the time it works. And then"—eraser tool again—"I go, Okay, I like that, so now I'm going to paint that. And then when I get it all to where I want, I go back to my original idea, and I'll, I'll do a glaze on top of this, and that'll push everything back, and then I can pull out what I want to show and what I don't want to show."

"What do you mean by 'paint that'?"

"Well, if you look through here, through the mirror at just what I did, if you can remember what it looked like before, this whole area has been closed in now, but it's still pushed back farther. My first point of view is going to be forefront, middleground, second middle ground, and distance, going all the way back. And, so I like what's going on here, so . . . then I'll take something—"

"We didn't just paint it?"

"No, I'm just drawing. I'll tell you: I think this is one of the best exercises I've ever had and to this day I work in that method. In elementary school, in *school*, instead of taking notes I would scribble and doodle. And that's kind of the same thing that I do now. I just go in and manipulate and turn things into"—he is applying some peach-colored paint to the right side of the new tree and to an indistinct area to the right of that, peach-colored paint that looks like the most inadvisable idea so far: what could be peach-colored in these woods, what could be peach-colored running all the way down the new tree, maybe it's salmon-colored, face-powder-colored, orange-popsicle-colored, *banana*-popsicle-colored—"the time of day where it's that late kind of light." And behold the new imprudent peach fucking up looks like sunlight coming through these dusky woods at approximately the horizontal, it is *sun*-colored paint I have been frightened by, and the new tree is lit by it, brilliantly and correctly. It's five thirty or six thirty or seven thirty in the Thomasville woods depending on your EST and your DST and the month.

Q: How many paintings do you do a year?

A: A lot.

Q: A hundred?

A: Almost.

Q: What do they sell for?

A: A small one, twenty-five to thirty-five—

Q: Twenty-five what?

A: Hundred.

Q: And a big one?

A: A big one? Well, several years ago I broke the six-figure mark.

C. Ford Riley gets the Subway tab. I offered, he counter-offered, I never participate in check fights. Ortega people might not understand this, but the girl who talked Bob Burns into quitting Lynyrd Skynyrd understands this.

I ask C. Ford Riley who his audience is and he says, "Welp . . ." and is understandably flummoxed.

"Ted Turner?"

"Ted has a large . . . amount."

C. Ford Riley explains that he has not met Ted Turner but that Ted Turner has bought a number of paintings. He says people like Turner are in another world; they fly private jets to Argentina on Saturday to hunt ducks and are at work Monday morning. I tell him that Ted Turner has just run off with the wife of a colleague of mine in the literary world, and that I had to remove Turner as a character in a book of mine putatively for legal reasons, and C. Ford Riley says Ted Turner gets in more trouble with his mouth, and that Ted Turner would not have sued about being in a book, and I say I know, and that he is not in trouble for running off with Bob Butler's wife, he just has Bob Butler's wife, and C. Ford Riley hands me a snapshot, saying "*Look* at that little son of a bitch."

In the photo are three men in camo clothes and camo makeup in a duck blind holding up so many ducks that their smiling faces are almost obscured and look like ducks themselves. Turner is in the middle, a happy man. If a Randall is the knife for people who want what C. Ford Riley can give them, and Thomasville is the epicenter of the good land, Ted Turner is the man, the quintessential man at the center of men claiming kinship with good land. In *Look at that little son of a bitch* is a tone of admiration that is broader and less literal than simple admiration. It is an admiration that looks in the mirror and is a broken chord and sees oneself there too, that looks at the land and the man who would own it, at a rich man who holds up ducks with the same glee as a poor man.

Down at the river we watch mullet jump in their playful-looking sawtooth leaps. The water is hot and flat and a tad muddy. C. Ford Riley throws a cast net on a small mullet and then the big ones get wary of the dock and of the men on it holding the blue net that would look to a mullet in the water like a man wearing a blue skirt. The almost necessary speculation as to why mullet jump begins: because they need extra oxygen (weak); because they like to play (fair); because, like dogs who lick themselves, *they can*. C. Ford Riley says, "I almost thought, once, they are looking for where to go."

We hie ourselves south to do some actual fishing on the Matanzas River. By rule when fishing with untested partner, C. Ford Riley sends me north in my kayak and he goes south in his; this way if I am a greenhorn I will not be a liability to him, only to myself. I am enough of a greenhorn that when I change bags as we launch I leave my nippers and have to chew through monofilament leaders to change lures, which takes so much time that when I see redfish tailing I refuse to change lures and I keep trying to get them to hit the Skitter Walk I have on instead of putting on a spoon, and when I get back I do not have a redfish and C. Ford Riley, who has put on a jig (he has put on, actually, a Berkley Gulp! New Penny Sans Plastique 100% Biodegradable three-inch shrimp that stinks to high heaven), has a redfish lashed to the side of his kayak that looks like a three-foot model submarine cruising with him. He's as proud as Ted Turner buried in ducks, and he's happy to say that he usually does not keep these fish, but exceptions have to be made, at points, and I agree. The best I can do is show him how to properly string a fish through the jaw not the gills. This is a down payment on the two paintings I will commission from him when my ship comes in.

In the picture I want of a mullet jumping, it is entirely likely he will put a tenable and readable expression on the mullet's face that suggests the mullet is looking for where to go. The other painting I want, and that I will entrust only to him, is of a redfish and a speckled trout together. These two fish are in certain ways the cat and dog of inshore salt water, one delicate- the other heavy-boned, one with scales hard to see and the other with scales like fingernails, one spotted many times and the other spotted usually once, one silver one copper, one coltish the other bullish, and they occupy nearly the same place on earth and do nearly the same thing (though a redfish can eat an oyster if it wants to and a trout may hurt its mouth on a sans plastique shrimp). The two fish constitute as strong an argument as there is for the brilliance of Darwin or God. If C. Ford Riley will paint them, the argument may tip one way or the other.

Bill Wegman

The first time I saw Bill Wegman, I think, I was on a porch over a lake in Maine at dusk and a fellow came paddling by in an aluminum canoe trolling a fly. I called to invite him up for a drink and was violently shushed by the people on the porch drinking. *He doesn't drink anymore*, it was imputed to me, and the implication obtained that his not drinking was a matter of such delicacy that were I to tempt him in the way I had Bill Wegman could be ruined. In this quiet corrected air on the porch I watched the interesting lone figure of Bill Wegman continue on his troubled way untroubled. He was wearing a funny-looking kepi with flies pinned to it and was sitting in the rear of the canoe. His weight tipped the front of the canoe way up in what is called, now, by me, the weather-vane configuration of canoes. Any woodsman is familiar with the weather-vaning of a canoe: the bow will swing downwind and you will go nowhere but downwind, if there is a wind. But there was no wind on Loon Lake and Bill Wegman went forward, having perhaps waved at me and my bad idea. The woman who had remonstrated the most against my hospitality had the largest breasts I had seen on a live human being and I would later learn that she had taken a man away from a friend of hers once, and the friend had, in revenge, flashed her own breasts at the large-breasted woman and screamed, "They're *real!*"

The large-breasted woman and the normal-breasted woman had been friends and waitresses some thirty years before at York's Lodge, a log affair so large that it had accommodated in the day the restaurant they worked in, a laundry, a lobby full of mounted big-game heads, some not from Maine, a fireplace a child could walk through without stooping, a boiler room, a library, a sitting porch facing the lake, a sitting porch not facing the lake, and even a machine to wash change, the kind of touch you hear about famous hotels in San Francisco having. The Lodge had served some fifteen or twenty cabins around it where the guests who ate at the restaurant and marveled at the animal heads and lounged and had their change washed stayed, and they were provided a newspaper and a fire in the mornings in these cabins by a boy. It was halcyon. By the time I saw any of it, it was gone. The Lodge was closed, the waitresses were flashing each other as old women, the sign in the Lodge that read No Jews or Consumptives was apparently offending no one, and the cabins had been sold off to individuals.

Bill Wegman at this point owned one of the cabins, called Sunset, in which he had photographed two Weimaraners in bed and called the photograph *Ray and Mrs. Lubner in Bed*. The close cabin and the cozy bed and the heavy bold plaid blankets and the logginess of everything, walls and furniture alike, were altogether so Maine-woods that even the perversion of two dogs looking like a happily married bourgeois couple in bed could not undo the Maine-woods kitsch. The Maine-woods kitsch in fact was enhanced by these goofing, Kinseyan dogs in bed. The Maine-woods kitsch, in fact, was no longer kitsch: these dogs in this bed made you want to be in the bed, own the cabin, be precisely in Maine, possibly even be in a happily married bourgeois couple. Were anyone else to put his dogs in bed it would look like dogs in bed. How did these dogs put there look like, well, something that had meaning? Who was this Bill Wegman dude?

Bill and I sat at the chipped white-enamel metal table in the kitchen of Sunset. I was in the fevery tremble of a hangover and I brought up the subject of my having invited his ruination by inviting him to have a drink so imprudently the other night as he weather-vaned by. Bill might have smiled. He told me that he had gone to Memphis once very drunk and remembered everything, and he had gone to Memphis sober and remembered nothing. This was just one of the sad ironies of living on the planet without booze. Bill did not say "the sad ironies of living on the planet without booze"; I thought it, trying to size up what the planet would be like as I steadily prepared to have to live on it myself. I was resisting the move. Bill said it was actually more fun after you made the move. Another improbable idea. Bill got on a Bakelite phone with a rotary dial and called a woman in New York, his girlfriend-assistant, and said, "Bring up a tube of that good red paint," paused, said, "A big one," and got off the phone. Then he said two women were going to visit and he'd had relations with both of them and this had never happened before and it might be weird. Ray and Mrs. Lubner's bed was right over there and there was no other bed and I had to agree. I thought maybe this Wegman dude was too New York for me, maybe too Paris. But he sounded like he was from California, or nowhere at all. And he was not going to utter the phrase "sad ironies" without more or less figuring out how to get a dog to say it. This much I knew so far.

So far I have intimated that I came to know Bill Wegman in a knowing, demonstrable, orderly, coherent, memorable way. I have been lying, and the exhaustion of lying now suggests I relax and just say a few things and admit that the things I have already presented are bogus here and there. The waitresses that worked in York's Lodge did in fact get in a fight over a man and the one who wore thick cat-eye glasses that she pushed up on her nose to keep them there who had lost the man did in fact show her breasts to and scream at the woman who stole the man. Once Bill Wegman and his painter friend David Deutsch walked into York's Lodge and read the sign that said No Jews or Consumptives, and David is Jewish and the woman with him had tuberculosis, and David and Bill thought it was funny. The two of them played around in Maine before Bill had reached the stage where he could acquire property, and of this time Bill says, "I was a complicated, messy person."

By the time I heard this I knew it was part of what we will call, very unWegmanly, the Wegman aesthetic. Complicated, even messy, ideas can be stated so simply that they have the sudden, surprising quality of truth, even if they are false. This is, to my mind, more or less what Bill Wegman is about. I'd rather not have to try to prove this right now, or give an example. Here's another stab at the idea: Bill Wegman takes oaf to the second power, where it is not oaf, and part of the way he does this is via line art as strong as that of Picasso and his bulls. Let's move on.

Maybe soon after I saw *Ray and Mrs. Lubner* and entertained my ideas about the planets Booze and Nobooze, etc., I saw a huge black-and-white photo of Bill's of a woman with a muscular back poised to throw a large tray, discus style. She looked like Arnold Schwarzenegger's sister if you are prepared to believe Arnold Schwarzenegger has a sister and that she'd be attractive. I probably received the notion (or made it up) that this woman was the girlfriend-assistant, or a previous girlfriend-assistant, and decided that Bill Wegman was not too New York or Paris for me but too *Tangier* if he's running with Schwarzenegger's sister and she's throwing Moroccan brass platters around nearly naked—this Wegman is an alpha dog, get away.

But Bill kept showing the oaf card. The Gap, I think, was going to come up and do a commercial with him in it; they were calling to see what size clothes to bring for the shoot. On the phone—now a mobile phone, on the porch of the Lodge, which he now owned—Bill said, "Me? I'm four foot nine and weigh four hundred *pounds.*" Another time he had consulted a doctor about pain in his lower back and the doctor, after ordering some X-rays, had come in and said, "I think we can rule out bone cancer." Bill was affronted by the indelicacy of the doctor's approach, and he said, "He came in and said, 'I think we can rule out BONE CANCER'"— virtually yelling *bone cancer*, the way he had virtually yelled *pounds* at the poor Gap girl. This is the technique, except here it is verbal: one word, one heightened word. In drawing and painting, it becomes one line, one correct line that does the work, the unique perfect meaning-making. Bill can find the line.

In all the dog stuff, he found the line by finding the *ur*-dog, the purest dogness of all the hundreds of breeds of dogs in the gray, elegant, unaffected, clean lines of the Weimaraner. I told Don Barthelme once that I had met Bill Wegman, asked what he thought of him. "Pretty good, but then the damn dog died." Bill ran around with John Belushi, and Belushi would taunt him, "Wegman! What you gonna do when the dog dies, Wegman!" When the dog died Wegman began breeding dogs.

So Bill Wegman over time went from one dog to five, six, seven dogs; from one cabin to that cabin, the Lodge, the tennis court, and the two houses opposite the Lodge; from one girlfriend-assistant bringing up a tube of red paint to a Ryder truck that spills out four people on payroll and klieg lights and cameras to make a movie, including a grip who can make a regulation tennis-umpire chair in a day and paint it the proper green. The last time I was in the studio they were deciding among designs for dog-print fabrics. It's an industry.

Yet it is not. You can still walk into the studio in Maine

and find Bill playing around with postcards, positioning
them on a board in order to seamlessly link them with a
paintbrush and paint, some of it red paint. Bill can paint.
He can very paint. I am past being struck by Mrs. Lubners
and dogs with elephant trunks on them and flour dumped
on them *perfectly* but I am not yet past the painting. That's
what you want to see. Ask to see the damned thing that was
walked on on the floor to prepare it—what do they call doing that?—that is based on little wild animals in Mexico.
Or, I don't know, has maybe one wild animal from Mexico
in it. Or has a fox, maybe just a fox, maybe it's a bat. Maybe
I am confusing the painting with a little booklet called *Wild
Animals of Mexico* I saw near the painting. Bill can paint.

Don Barthelme

Don Barthelme once said to me, "The trouble with teaching is you spend all your time working on someone else's rotten manuscript when you should be working on your own rotten manuscript." This is signature Barthelme. It contains the making of a joke by repeating two syllables or two words or two phrases, at which he was very good: "And I sat there getting drunker and drunker and more in love and more in love." Sometimes the two words are so good you do not repeat them for the joke to obtain. One night Don's wife, Marion, reported, not without a tinge of worry, that the neighbor's dog had nipped their child. Don said, "Does she warrant it not *rabid*?" *Warrant* and *rabid* had not been heard in a while; their archaic novelty was funny and gently suggested we not worry overmuch in our modern bourgeois fatted travail. "Does it have rabies?" would not have managed this humoring balm. Another time Marion reported that a strange young man had come to the door, vaguely menacing somehow—"Did he have a *linoleum knife* in his *pocket*?" Don said, nearly laughing himself.

"Rotten manuscript" also contains his careful self-deprecation. The repetition surprises twice: we do not

anticipate a prudent teacher's calling a student's manuscript
rotten, and we certainly do not anticipate Don Barthelme's
calling his own manuscript rotten. He was always prudent
to not promote himself in just this way. If he praised himself, he detracted, and the praise was seen to have been but a
setup. One night he said, "I am going to read a story called
'Overnight to Many Distant Cities,' a lovely title I took
from the side of a postal truck." This capacity, this tendency
to what he called "common decency," lifted him from the
mortal street where he was a pioneer writer—arguably, I
think, one who began with "bad Hemingway" (cf. *Paris Review* interview) and refracted that through Kafka and Beckett and Perlman and Thurber and changed the aesthetic of
short fiction in America for the second half of the twentieth
century in equal measure to the way Hemingway changed
it in the first, and Twain before that—well, from this high
mortal street to, in my eyes at least, a kind of high mortal deity. Don was God here in Houston, loved by some of us and
not by others, like all gods, and if he was not always godly he
was always goodly to us. He was a Biggie and he was goodly.
He was a strange New York Biggie who was, even more
strangely, *from here*, and he was back with some benevolent
plan. It had a powerful effect. We were lowly sun-addled
Aztecs to his Quetzalcoatl, and it felt like we'd been waiting
for him a long time without knowing it.

In my own case we entered into a special affair when I
discovered by accident that if you demanded good fathering of him, he who spent a third of his time writing about
bad fathering, a phrase he considered redundant, he would

oblige you. The day we met him, he came up on Glenn Blake and me to shake hands and trapped us in tiny school desks we couldn't get out of quickly. We struggled to get up and stand as boys with proper manners would—here came Andy Warhol, in an urban-cowboy suit, on a slight vodka tilt, bearing down on us, and we'd better stand up. He saw us trying to be good boys (he did not see that we were caught so flat-footed because our previous teacher here would not have deigned shake hands with us). Within a few weeks I was saying to him in a manuscript conference, "Don't you *ever* withhold a comment from me. I am not here to be coddled. I came here to meet women. And I am not going to write a thesis. If I have to do this I am going to write *a book*." "By all means," Don Barthelme said, chuckling, closing the manuscript, both of us chuckling. A boy demanding more rigor, not less, of a father! A man who theretofore felt all fathering tantamount to botching and bullying! We gave it a try. I have said all this tonight because I did not say any of it at the funeral. I avoid funerals and weddings.

I am going to read a Barthelme story. The trouble with reading someone else's story is that you have spent all your time reading your own stories messing them up and no time reading someone else's stories messing them up. It makes you nervous in a new way, especially against the chance that some of you might have heard Don Barthelme mess up reading his own stories. That was some powerful, crisp, deft, nuanced, trippingly enunciated, princely timed messing up that made you laugh not only at that which had not struck you as funny when you read it, but at that which you had not even sometimes understood. On a night when he had asked if the neighbor's dog was warranted to be not rabid, or if the boy at the door carried a knife, this story—the story I am going to mess up reading—was handed to me in manuscript by Don Barthelme, who said, "Here. My latest." He was showing me how it actually worked, or *that* it actually worked. When we saw one of his stories in *The New Yorker* we thought it had sprung full-blown from on high. I was to see that it started on unspoiled paper and you spoiled the paper by typing very neatly with good margins and no mess and sent it to Roger Angell and *then* it looked the way it looked in *The New Yorker*. The paper was spoiled on that typewriter over there by the door where the boy with the linoleum knife and the boy who had disappointed us by not having a linoleum knife had tried to gain entry. There were water marks from the stem of a glass on the wood by the typewriter.

Flannery O'Connor

A Craft Talk Without Craft

I am thinking tonight, as I address this unenviable task, of Flannery O'Connor, because she would advise against it, my addressing this unenviable task. I revere her in a way that she would also advise against, in fact would probably repudiate outright, hard: as something of the godhead, or goddesshead, of letters. I like touching the goddesshead. I do it whenever I can. I'll touch the godhead too. Once I was so drunk on the grounds of Faulkner's famous home, Rowan Oak, and a storm hit so violently that I was convinced Wash Jones would come out of the house with the scythe and I would not hear him for the thunder and only at the last minute in a flash of lightning would I see him with the weapon poised to behead me, which I deserved.

I call Flannery's cousin Louise Florencourt sometimes to touch the goddesshead. Louise is nine months younger than Flannery would be were she alive, and regally correct (she was one of the first three women to attend Harvard

Law School, in 1937), and never married, and is Catholic, and is literary executrix of her famous cousin's estate, and lives right there in Milledgeville in her famous cousin's mother's big house on Greene Street so fine that it once served as the temporary governor's mansion, and Louise still has a mule, Flossie, on the famous farm, a hennie mule that was almost there when Flannery was, or maybe was there, mules live forever and my arithmetic is weak and I have not asked Louise if Flossie and Flannery actually overlapped, so Louise is to my mind the closest thing, genotypically and phenotypically, to Flannery O'Connor, and when I talk to Louise I feel it's as close as it's going to get to talking to Flannery, touching the goddesshead.

Sometimes Louise quietly rebukes, and that is thrilling. Once at her country club at lunch I told her of my recent divorce and she presumed I would be in some kind of rebound peril and she said, "You have to be very careful, Mr. Powell. Of course I'm too old." I froze the way I imagine one does when playing cards in a saloon and you are accused of cheating.

I feel I may have gotten a little off-line. Maybe I should say here that I think the craft of fiction has a lot more to do with being off-line than with being on-line, a whole lot more, but in saying that I would be appreciably more off-line than I wish to be at this juncture. I have not even properly detailed yet why this task is unenviable and why in its particulars I am reminded of Flannery O'Connor. I have intimated that these are things I will say, and one of the things fiction must do, I am afraid, is deliver what is intimated will be delivered. Here is Flannery O'Connor, then, if you must have it, on the giving of advice, and why I am calling the giving of advice unenviable:

"I am becoming convinced that anybody who gives anybody else advice ought to spend forty days in the desert both before and after."

My arithmetic is not so weak that I cannot figure that to be eighty days in the desert. That is too much. I have no experience with the desert but I spent thirty-seven days on the ground in Kenya, as opposed to in the safari car where mzungu is advised to stay, and was so debilitated by what the French doctor attending my survival called an intestinal weerus after we spent three months looking for a parasite that could not be found by every blood test there is, and stool analysis, and finally sonogram, which altogether I estimate would have cost about $10,000 in the States but that ran me $250 in France, so please do not tell me that we do not want a public option or that socialized medicine is evil—was so debilitated by the weerus that I found Jesus, or He me, walking along a quay on a midwinter day in sunny Bretagne.

Jesus I now know, though Flannery would cane me for this, is the invisible friend that we tell children after age five they may not have. He will pull you through, even through a weerus from Africa. My Jesus wears a Pink Panther suit dirty at the knees.

Where are we? I am braving the eighty days, then, because Ben Marcus has offered me some of Columbia's money to do so, and I am a good boy who meets his contractual obligations. I was a good boy as a boy and wanted to attend to my intellectual fundament by coming to Columbia but my mother would not fill out the financial disclosure that would have secured the necessary aid and so I did not come, and divorced my mother, and did not, as you can already glean, ever attend to my intellectual fundament. Another good boy who had trouble with his mother but who did manage to come to New York, whether to attend to his intellectual fundament or not, with whom I was familiar as I struggled against mothers and want of intellection, is Tennessee Williams. I flunked out of chemistry school by reading everything Tennessee Williams wrote instead of organic chemistry, and a kind of early mother-in-law gave a party for him in Charleston and did not tell me, and while in Charleston, to premier one of those late failed plays you can learn so much more from than from the earlier well-made plays, just as you can see how and why Hemingway was so good only by reading him after he had lost his mind, Tennessee Williams bought a safari suit out of the window of Dumas & Sons on King Street, and it is said he wore it for the duration of his time in Charleston, which I estimate at two weeks. Tennessee Williams drunk and in his stained khaki suit and I was not invited! Fortunately that girl got rid of me and that got rid of that kind of early mother-in-law who did not invite me. I once inadvertently saw her freshly showered, and she had powdered what Butters on *South Park* calls bush with heavy talc so that it looked a ghostly white over black, an unappetizing pastry as it were, and once that daughter who would so prudently later get rid of me caught her taking acid and slapped her. You all have probably heard that Tennessee Williams when he got so suddenly rich and famous in fancy New York hotels mistook chocolate sauce for gravy and poured it on his steak and broke the arms to sofas and so forth. It was behavior of that sort, on top of my having read all the bad formative work and the good work and the later thrilling deteriorating work, while being declared a failure at chemistry school, which would make me then have to be a roofer, which among other transgressions would have that girl biochemist get rid of me, and me her Bermuda Triangle mother, that made me really want to meet Tennessee Williams. I would have had nothing to say of interest to him sitting there in a giant wing chair in his fouled khaki with the ludicrous fond epaulettes. I was then as pretty as a girl so maybe he would have been interested in me had I said nothing at all, but I'd not have had the wit for that.

Here is what I hope with everything I have left in me I would not have said: Mr. Williams, I am a roofer in Texas because I read all your stuff and I am honing my craft. I would not be mortified today had I said: Mr. Williams, I am a roofer in Texas because I read all your stuff. Ms. O'Connor's Hazel Motes, whom I trust all of you know, or know of, put it this way: "I've started my own church . . . The Church Without Christ." Nabokov has his famous bitchy roosterism about the worst thing a student can say to him is that he, the student (and he probably meant right here at Columbia), has "a lot of ideas"; for me, rivaling Nabokov for bitchery and failing in every other measure to even get on scale (for example, my speaking a second language I now concede will depend upon the Language Fairy's putting one under my pillow), the last thing I want to hear, ever, and a thing for which I will dismiss a petitioner outright who seeks study anywhere near me, is the phrase "hone my craft." I would rather hear "spank my monkey." In fact it is reasonably likely that I will admit an applicant avowing that he seeks to spank his monkey if he can manage some slight elegance or surprise or deprecation to indicate that maybe he understands how likely it is that the pursuit of writing is so often naught *but* a spanking of one's monkey, and sometimes someone else's monkey. I have used the masculine pronoun in the construction of this silly conceit not in a spirit of sexism but because I hoped some elegance might redeem the silliness and because women are not commonly thought of in connection with monkey spanking. Be assured that with equal ardor I do not want a woman to tell me she wants to hone her craft.

People, we have started our craft talk, the Craft Talk Without Craft. It has been a prodigious introduction and it remains to be seen if a talk can ensue at all. I am weak from fear of the desert.

I am now going to proffer some little things that may combine in your mind to mean something, or not. They may mean something discretely, or not. They may combine better in an order I do not have the wit to determine, but that is okay, since you are having to hear them in the air where they are already subject to the Brownian motion of podium slur and so are already combining in the weird indeterminate order of the misheard and the partially heard. I grasped Brownian motion before flunking out of chemistry school. Had the mother-in-law who powdered herself so prodigiously spilled talc into the toilet, a distinct possibility given the liberality of the dusting of her cruller, you could have seen the talc move on the toilet water in what is called Brownian motion. If there is calculus to describe Brownian motion I mercifully flunked out still innocent of it. That one can even now utter the clause "if there is calculus" is an indicator of supreme naivete because there is calculus to describe everything, which is why, aside from reading Mr. Williams when I was supposed to read Mr. Morrison and Mr. Boyd, I flunked out of chemistry school. I am going on about this now not merely because of my giant reluctance to start the Craft Talk Without Craft but also because remaining innocent of things is in my view an important part of writing, which will become clear if I ever start the talk.

Here then are seven utterances by six more or less smart people that taken together form a manifesto for deintellectualizing the approach to craft, or for admitting that it is but spanking the monkey, one's or someone else's:

> 1) My best stories come out of nowhere, with no concern for form at *all*.
> —Barry Hannah
> 2) I can take a sentence apart and tell you

why I did it; obviously that's the key to the whole thing, being able to write a sentence, and I've got a sense of what my sentences ought to do.   —Pete Dexter

3) Learn to play your instruments, then get sexy.   —Debbie Harry

4) Some people run to conceits or wisdom but I hold to the hard, brown, nut-like word. I might add that there is enough aesthetic excitement there to satisfy anyone but a damned fool.

   —Donald Barthelme (character)

5) There is at the back of every artist's mind something like a pattern or a type of architecture. The original quality in any man of imagination is imagery. It is a thing like the landscape of his dreams; the sort of world he would like to make or in which he would wish to wander; the strange flora and fauna of his own secret planet; the sort of thing he likes to think about. This general atmosphere, and pattern or structure of growth, governs all his creations, however varied.

   —G. K. Chesterton

6) Anyway, when I told you to write what was *easy* for you, what I should have said was what was *possible* for you.

   —Flannery O'Connor

7) Art is not difficult because it wishes to be
difficult but because it wishes to be art.
—Donald Barthelme (himself)

If I may presume to boil down the podium slur and con-
dense these positions: the larger scheme of things will take
care of itself if you will be sure to locate the right next hard
brown nut-like word. Play your instrument, the sentence,
before getting sexy with conceits and wisdom. Your notion
of form, if you have one, is safely in the back of your mind,
the landscape of your dreams, and it will out as you struggle
with what is possible for you to struggle with, the words. Let
things become difficult on their own, if they so insist (and
they may not), without your deliberate help.

I saw Allen Collins become a world-class sexy rock star
advancing the conceits of a psychedelic band with the wisdom to masquerade as the redneck band Lynyrd Skynyrd. I
watched him learn to play his guitar in the eighth grade with
an amp so small he could put his foot on it to play better.
When he was not suspended he was aimlessly walking the
halls of junior high school. He did not want to be a rock star,
he wanted to be a good guitar player. He became that, and
then he became the other.

It has taken us a long time to get here, and I confess I am as
tired of this as you are. I feel like taking a pill and speeding
things up. If any of you has any synthetic narcotics please
see me before I enter the desert. I would now like to debunk
craft books.

As a child, even before I reached the flunking-out-of-science stage, I glanced at some craft books. I even still own some, in particular a thin volume called, pertinently, I presume, *The Craft of Fiction*, by Percy Lubbock, whose name I love, but whose book alas I have not opened. I do remember actually opening *The House of Fiction* by Caroline Gordon, who ran with Allen Tate and Randall Jarrell and Peter Taylor and took counsel from Andrew Lytle and gave it to Flannery O'Connor. In this book were complicated diagrams having to do with point of view, I think; they featured a circle and an arrow. The arrow might come just to the circle, like common sperm, or it might penetrate the circle, like the putatively lucky one, and these relative positions of the arrow had to do with matters of omniscience, and limited omniscience, and so forth—who could, appropriately, conceive what. A diagram of the benzene ring with its famous resonating bonds was by contrast more intelligible than these pictures, and that is one reason I pursued chemistry as opposed to English in college. Another reason is that I could not write a critical paper on, say, assonance and dissonance in the ballads of Thomas Campion without getting a D because, one professor told another, ending my English majoring the day I learned of it, I did not *believe* in the paper. Which was true; it was a parody of an English paper, but it was more astute than the non-parodies in the room. I *could* reproduce the mathematical argument that any given particle can be, at some probable moment, on the backside of the moon without getting a D. This argument I also had trouble believing but I was not, in the chemistry department, punished for skepticism.

In these books, these craft books, then, you will also find bloviations on terms such as *exposition*, which means a fair in which goods or wares or scientific and cultural wonders are displayed to the public; round characters and flat characters; backstory; rising action, crisis, climax, denouement, detumescence; theme; metaphor; the difference between the ambivalent, a good thing, and the ambiguous, a bad thing; the bastardizing of telling versus the apotheosis of showing, hands down the largest bogosity of them all; and the existence of the necessary inevitable which necessarily cannot be anticipated before its inevitability becomes apparent. I will feel better going into the desert whether I have pills from you or not if you will all give me assurances that you will never, ever, give a thought to any of these ephemera above, except that if you think you can make a flat character I would like to see a whole book of *really flat characters* in it and I would like you to mail it to me in the desert. Promise me that you will never say to anyone that you wanted to establish a "close third." Promise me that you will never use the term, or think that you are covertly rendering, an "unreliable narrator." Nor may you entertain that there is some kind of subtle difference between a narrator and an author. There is only a huge difference, so the matter of the difference need not be entertained except by obvious and dim people from whom we need not hear, aside from me.

The nineteen rules, some say twenty-two, governing the art of romantic fiction that Twain laid out in his dismembering of Fenimore Cooper you may use. Of particular value are Use the right word, not its second cousin, followed hard by Eschew surplusage. Twain has, as genius does, anticipated by fifty years and bettered by one word William Strunk's more common and pedestrian and second-cousinly and surplussey Omit needless words. Forget the hokum that adjectives are second-class citizens. Without adjectives you can't have no second-class citizens, or first-. You must resist arrant nonsense.

Man, I like the oxycodone without the aspirin affixed to it. The aspirin is the damage-doer. I wish Jimi Hendrix would walk in here and end this. Strunk and White have another famous bogus rule: Place the emphatic words at the end of the sentence. Let us accept for the moment that some words are inherently more emphatic by themselves than others, even if the argument is tenuous. Is *cut throat* more emphatic or less emphatic than *sanguinary demise*? Is *harbinger* more emphatic than *hint*? Is *bastard* more emphatic than *shiftless character*? Is *siren* more emphatic than *pretty girl*, really? But for the hell of it let's say rock breaks scissors. Now, what Strunk and White mean, of course, is that the words at the end of a sentence *are* emphatic, the ones that are emphasized, and this is a useful notion. Presumably, then, the words not at the end are not emphasized as much. Now look at this, which I will read in a distracting if not deliberately comic manner to emphasize the relevant words, by which I mean words that are repeated but in positions of differing emphasis:

> Mrs. May's bedroom window was low and faced on the east and the bull, silvered in the moonlight, stood under it, his *head raised* as if he listened—like some patient god come down to woo her—for a stir inside the room. The window was dark and the sound of her breathing too light to be carried outside. Clouds crossing the moon blackened him and in the dark he began to tear at the hedge. Presently they passed and he appeared again in the same spot, *chewing steadily*, with a hedge-wreath that he had ripped loose for himself caught in the tips of his *horns*. When the moon drifted into retirement again, there was nothing to mark his place but the *steady* sound of his *chewing*. Then abruptly a pink glow filled the window. Bars of light slid across him as the venetian blind was slit. He took a step backward and *lowered his head* as if to show the wreath across his *horns*.

That is Miss O'Connor holding to the hard brown nut-like word. She is eschewing the conceit and wisdom that Mrs. May is the most presumptuous woman in Georgia if not in the world and that her presumption will merit this bull's goring her to death. But she is discovering it, and telling it, and building the necessary inevitable that is not supposed to be apparent. Here are the repeated words, in order: *head raised, chewing steadily, horns, steady chewing, lowered head, horns.*

Miss O'Connor was paying attention to the word, and she had a sense of what her sentences ought to do: "Bars of light slid across him as the venetian blind was slit" is not "Mrs. May opened the blinds and bars of light slid across the bull."

She can hardly contain the outrage inspired in her by Mrs. May. She is eager to get going on the portrait that will make us celebrate with her the violent undoing of this kind of person. Mrs. May next dismisses the bull as "Some [n-word's]* scrub bull," then this:

> Green rubber curlers sprouted neatly over
> her forehead and her face beneath them was
> smooth as concrete with an egg-white paste
> that drew the wrinkles out while she slept.

We will watch much happen to Mrs. May as she sleeps, and in fact not until the bull gores her does she wake: "[S]he had the look of a person whose sight has been suddenly restored but who finds the light unbearable."

•

* Editor's replacement.

Write like that. Herewith is concluded the Craft Talk Without Craft. I would assess it so far a failure. I have attempted in its method, as opposed to its message—that is to say, I have attempted in the preaching itself rather than in the content of the sermon—to instruct all that I am qualified to instruct: that writing is controlled whimsy. Force whimsy just enough to make sense. How much force does that require? Good question.

There are martial-arts enthusiasts in the room, or at least one. Hello, Lieutenant Wilson. I myself have endured enough dojo and kwoon, in which, the kwoon, one frequently holds a position called horse long enough to stave off terminal old-man butt well enough that perfectly correct women like Louise Florencourt are compelled to tell you they are too old, and a certain kind of less correct middle-aged woman is compelled to freshen the accusation that one is in the throes of the mid-life crisis, which accusation this certain kind of middle-aged woman apparently takes more pleasure in issuing each time she utters it—where are we? Where we are is I am demonstrating not enough force upon the whimsy.

In the kung-fu kwoon it is paramount that in a fight one remain loose; this is arguably the martial-arts equivalent to the NRA safety rule #1 that you Always Point the Gun in a Safe Direction, which, alas, proves the only rule necessary. In kung fu the big and necessary rule is Remain Loose, and the neophytes and the seekers of the grandfather's wisdom keep asking, How loose? And the answer is, "Well, grasshopper, not exactly a noodle." You must place enough force upon your whimsy that it is not exactly a noodle.

Your conceit—your plan, your regrettable *ideas* (it is useful to think of O'Connor's calling herself "a writer innocent of theory but not without certain preoccupations")—as you write cannot be so fixed, so brittle that it break in the event your imagination delivers a surprise. Nor can it be a mush of overcooked inane sentiment. *Al dente*, then, a noodle between brittle and mush, a chewy substance, allows accidents of utterance that may have unintentional consequences, happy and unhappy. I should not have revealed that I have had an intimate-seeming lunch in Milledgeville, but alas I did, as one thing led to another.

All of this is about the power of repetition, which is but emphasizing words to the second power. All writing is the right word, the right position of the word, and the right position of the word to the second power, its repetition. All of this is but Making Sense, the big and necessary *only rule* in writing. It is the equivalent, clearly, to Always Pointing the Gun in a Safe Direction and to Remaining Loose, but not as loose as a noodle.

I feel fine. I have acquitted myself handsomely and neatly, by accident, the only way neatness is palatable. I have failed most in not detailing exactly what Tennessee Williams looked like in the large chair, an overstuffed wing chair in the parlor of a Charleston single house, sitting weirdly aslant, in his dirty safari suit, resembling a tiny mad king looking around the room for young men drawn to his celebrity, for me, who was not there. As Mr. Williams himself was to put it, the future becomes the present, the present becomes the past, and the past is filled with eternal regret.

Goodbye. You will not see me again, unless you yourselves are compelled to give advice and join me in the desert. Bring the pills.

Grace Paley

By no reckoning of a real clock or of real life did I know Grace Paley well. Yet I felt, and I suspect this phenomenon is not unknown to many who knew her a little, that we were intimate. As she would have said, or might have had a character say: this was maybe not my fault altogether. She came on to you, to continue the business of her comic habit of putting things bluntly and inaccurately for a truthful effect. She came on to you with the gum chewing and the smile and the electric eyes and the wild hair and the offer, without extending her hand one inch, to hold hands with you.

Once this started obtaining, say across the room, you first decided she should be your grandmother. Then your mother. Then your wife. But she was too old for that. You thought of where in her stories Faith recalls having been a hottie in her day, or some gumpy old fart like Zagrowsky decides she was a hottie in her day, and you can tell that someone really was hot, it's not a fiction, whether the character is a fiction or not someone in this picture was a hottie all right, and it was Grace. So now you have this sexy grandmother mothering you somehow, tacitly, whose hand you want to take, for reasons of the security of mothering, which is somehow being offered, even though almost no direct attention is being paid you. She's just chewing gum and saying that so-and-so's doing this or doing that, with outsized passion, which exceeds need, is dumb. She may not be saying something or someone is dumb. She needn't be saying anything at all. She's just in the room, ready with her presence alone to say, Settle down, boys, and thereby stop a fuss or a riot, and she has the quiet power to do it. The power seems to inhere in her chewing gum and saying whatever it is she will say without an extra syllable or a prettifier or softener of any sort. I was wanting to write "stool softener" right there as a joke but that is exactly the kind of joke, or showing off, that Grace Paley abjured, and that made her writing work, and that made this calming, soothing effect of her character work, too.

Once, somehow the subject of Norman Mailer's misbehavior came up, perhaps with respect to Grace and PEN, I can't recall, and perhaps I was teasing her and saying Norman was going to get her, or something to that effect, and she said, "No, he's too old and sick." Whatever the conversation had been went on in stride, but I stopped and regarded this sentence and the person who said it and how she said it. Let us say that Grace is by then getting some orange juice from Marion Barthelme and they are talking about someone or something I am not a part of. The kitchen is sunny and they have their girl business and their juice. I was free to regard "No, he's too old and sick," referring as it does to an early writer hero of mine and uttered by a later hero, a writer of an entirely different kind, a kind that one in fact cannot

even imagine while enamored as a teenager of writers like
Norman Mailer.

The hidden sentiments that Grace did not say but that
made the phenomenon of Grace Paley and that made you
want to hold her hand or hope she'd take your hand are in
italics: *Oh, Norman and I go back a ways, sometimes nasty, usually
okay, he's combative but really sweet, like all of you he's just a boy being*
boys, *he won't be troubling me now, or anyone, I'm afraid*, no, he's
too old and sick, *bless his heart.*

You heard in "No, he's too old and sick," the six little
words that actually came out of her, without all the excelsior
I have supplied, that Norman's a sport, he's okay. A mother
does not disown. The six words said: If we have Grace, we
have a mother, there she is getting some orange juice, thank
God. Settle down.

At other times I recall her suggesting that Donald Barthelme's early death clearly owed to his smoking and drinking to excess, which she attributed to machismo and I think
called "silly." Here it was again: men will be boys. Men insist
on being boys. Men *are* boys. One can find many a woman
to dispense this sentiment, you'll need not strain yourself
turning over rocks to find them, but I submit it is rare to
find one saying it with only a hint of vexation and a large
heart full of understanding, if not a soupçon of fellow-
traveler glee. "He was silly," she says, smacking the gum, her
eyes as bright as fried marbles. At this moment it is tenable
that Grace Paley is herself a boy, a tired boy. She won't as a
boy throw in and vote to ban girls from the tree fort, no, but
she will raise some funds for the tree fort, and she is going

to climb up there with you even if you ban her, smiling and seeing that a better time is had up there than if it is just the boys up there. That was Grace Paley, to the best of my hazarding: a boy. A literary boy who'd been a hot woman and who had had children and who took care of men and what of the world she could.

Lena Padgett, Nan Morrison

Women Who Lead You to Books

I had an aunt whose husband died in WWII and who played poker and smoked and drank and took very good casual care of me. She was the only relative of mine of whom I can say I was fond. She gave me back scratches, and not short ones, with heavy red fingernails, and we popped popcorn in a sauce-pot on the stove so inexpertly and negligently that the popped corn always lifted the lid off and went all over the kitchen. If she had asked, and if I had not already become the bourgeois snot I was to become, I'd have run away with her. This is all tangentially related to the first book that spoke to me.

In my aunt's bookshelf, filled with paperbacks of the high-acid prematurely brown type, which seemed to be love westerns, or something at any rate that did not interest me, I one day discovered, in a mass edition already brown itself, and looking from its spine *almost* like a love western, Norman Mailer's *Advertisements for Myself.* I opened it and knew instantly I was in the presence of something radical—not merely not a love western, but not a love western to the second or third power. The high italics count was spooky, electric-looking. These were the passages *about* the writing, not the writing itself (the second power), and scanning with my early testosterone radar I spied sodomy and things (the third power) and secreted the book away.

I studied it. Mailer was a man who went around writing, "Like many another vain, empty, and bullying body of our time, I have been running for President these last ten years in the privacy of my mind . . . ," and who found insupportable the role of nice Jewish boy from Brooklyn. I was finding insupportable, I suppose, the role of nice *goy* boy afraid to run away with his aunt, which I hadn't thought of, and who wasn't going to propose it, anyway, but I was finding *something* insupportable, or I wouldn't have waited out those purple, electric sentences, and I wouldn't have thought it a cool thing to call oneself a vain and bullying body of our time.

I took Mailer at his word: you advertise *yourself* to become a writer, and not surprisingly I then read what might be called celebrity authors—Capote, Vidal, Tennessee Williams: writers who spent a visible portion of themselves talking about writing or themselves or themselves as writers, or, *viz.*, Mailer and Vidal, fighting about writing. As I studied this celebrity I became aware of a spectrum toward its obverse: for a Mailer there was, say, a Roth, then a Bellow; and, well, you have the picture.

The second book that spoke to me—an asinine locution: I mean that hissed or yelled at me, frightened me—was also, I realize now, provided me by a woman who smoked and drank and took very good casual care of me, though this was a careful and deliberate professional casualness, and she was the only English professor of whom it may be said I was ever fond. I was at her house late one night and revealed—apropos of what, I cannot fathom, but in the general atmosphere of my having threatened her with my being not a mere stooge of her classroom criticism (it was late, and I was mixing the drinks, her sane husband had retired), and in the general atmosphere of her having promised me that she would be my mentor, then, if I would write—that I had never read Faulkner.

"What?"

She was out of her chair and gone and back, dropping in my lap a Modern Library *Absalom, Absalom!* with, I noticed, opening it, her maiden name on the flyleaf. In that mysterious sequence of events which conspires to make a boy a writer—facts and forces that are anybody's guess and are always tedious if anybody starts the guessing—this was a heavyweight moment.

"I am appalled."

I could only chuckle, because she *was.* Here I was, unread and unready, proclaiming I would write, and here she was, read and ready to coach in a mission that was holy, and I the supplicant had not read the Scripture. What miracle prevented her throwing me out of the house? The hour, the booze, the novelty of a boy who would so presume? Was she bored by the correct boys at school?

I was partly in love—a literary mother! but sort of not a mother! (that maiden name contained a magic suggestion—a *woman* was taking notice of me)—and I was in possession of the Word. The tissuey pages of the book, the tight type, the "Absalom!"—whatever that meant—the gift was mystical in my hand. This was as close to a religious experience as I am likely to suffer on Earth.

As had happened to me with the actual Bible, I began to try to read this weirdly holy book, and couldn't. But I had a secular mother non-mother looking over my shoulder, not the dubious authority of Protestantism. I read to page 60 or so of *Absalom, Absalom!* four or five times, as I recall. Each time I stalled out like a car going up a hill.

Somehow on one of the uphill runs I made it to page 100 or so, and then began the breathtaking downhill seduction, the rush, the delightful surrender to fictive gravity, and I was not the same boy when I finished the book. I could not have explicated the thing (could not today), did not know who said what to whom two percent of the time, and yet was entirely aboard the Dixie Limited, as I would learn later Flannery O'Connor called him. How could something so preposterously private be remotely public? How could the book-club ladies who objected to the "difficulty" be at once correct and not correct? How—alas, who cares?

I would then read about a third of the *oeuvre*, using as a springboard a copy of the Viking *Portable Faulkner* which I never returned to the local county library, and which I yet have as I negotiate an amnesty with them which will allow me to come in safely against my prodigious, twenty-five-year, $37,500 fine. I stopped there (in the reading, at a third of the Faulkner corpus; the fine presumably mounts yet). Any more Faulkner, I felt, and I would not dare presume write myself. Any more evidence of this Olympic steam a boy they called Bill or Count No Count could learn to blow and there would be no point attempting to make steam myself.

In order not to give up, Walker Percy (I regard Percy the child of Flannery O'Connor and Faulkner) is a good homeopathic cure against dying of Faulkneritis. This drinking mothering professor of mine also introduced me to Percy. She found *The Moviegoer* a tad "cute," at variance with the prevailing opinion of the day. I was more attracted to the more or less openly "flawed" *The Last Gentleman*, which made me want to be its hero for a good solid three weeks, an improvement, aesthetically speaking, to wanting to be Norman Mailer.

Denis Johnson

For the Denis Johnson Memorial
October 2, 2017, NYC

I am writing this from Florida, where my house has just been flooded by Hurricane Irma. If you have trouble following me it is because I will have trouble composing. My marbles are scattered all over the floor, and the floor recently had eighteen inches of swamp water on it. A lesser or greater siren—a swamp amphibian—swam by me in the kitchen, just before I blew up the stove trying to cook eggs for the boys who helped me hump the furniture to the second floor. I did not go to hospital with burnt hand only because I'd have had to swim, in the dark, with a burnt hand. None of this is relevant. What is relevant is that Denis is gone. *Focus*, Powell.

A natural literary law is that the ardor with which an editor asks for a blurb is in inverse proportion to the chances that he or she will use the blurb. I am no longer able to write a blurb that will be used on a book. My latest rejected blurb, for a book called *The Australian* by Emma Smith-Stevens, went like this:

The central figure here, the titular Australian, is unmanned with a quiet, wise, sure-
footed humor that is winning and subtle
and seductive. Condensing this sentiment
to its second-class citizens, Ms. Smith-
Stevens is quiet, wise, sure-footed, winning,
subtle, and seductive.

"Condensing this sentiment to its second-class citizens"
tries to refer to the bromide that adjectives are not first-class
words like nouns and verbs. I thought I was pretty clever
in whacking that idiocy en route to praising the book with
good adjectives. Ms. Smith-Stevens wrote me quickly:

My editor was wondering if we could kind
of combine the two sentences to read like
this:
    Ms. Smith-Stevens, like the titular Aus-
tralian, is unmanned with a quiet, wise,
sure-footed humor that is winning and subtle and seductive.

I wrote Ms. Smith-Stevens more quickly that I did not
think her editor could seriously want me to say that she, a
girl, or a woman, as you choose, could be unmanned, even
by her own book, or especially by her own book, which presumably the editor, who had bought it, liked.

After some back and forth, for which Ms. Smith-Stevens

apologized, and which apology I accepted because she was—
full disclosure—a student of mine and I wanted to help her,
we (they) arrived at this for the book jacket:

> *The Australian* is unmanned with a quiet,
> wise, sure-footed humor that is winning
> and subtle and seductive.

Dumb blurb in the can! All right. Now I am ready to
focus. Thirty-one years ago when Denis Johnson and I won
Whitings together he told *The New York Times*, when asked
what he would do with the money, "I'm going to buy me one
of them genius pigs." That alerted me to the possibility of
the presence of wit. I looked at *Angels* and *Fiskadoro*—a book
I have heard but do not credit he wanted later to disown; I
want to steal the Vietnamese woman floating in the ocean
for four days—and decided Denis Johnson was *the* competition. And then *Jesus' Son* came in the mail asking me for a
blurb. From I think FSG, where I was walking the plank.
I sat down, marshaled the marbles, which I could do then,
bore down as hard as I can with my pencil, made a muscle
with my head, and wrote:

> Mr. Johnson takes loss through some kind
> of sound barrier, past which celebrations of
> joy in destitution appear. For clean line, for
> deftness, for hard honest comedy there is no
> better than Denis Johnson.

The blurb was accepted as I wrote it, *mirabile dictu*. Perhaps because no one could say it not true. I am yet proud of the two-adjective one-noun phrase "hard honest comedy," and that is what I am sticking to, and that is why I have labored on like this from soggy Florida with all my shit ruint to tender the highest praise I can with respect to writing and with respect to a writer: the best is *hard honest* comedy, and Denis Johnson was the *best* at it.

Just go look at those squished baby rabbits again.

Spode

I have been writing about my dog, I discover, for twenty-two years, twice as long as he lived and he dead now eighteen years. What would compel a man who fancies himself unsentimental and sane to such a thing? The dog, moreover, was also unsentimental and sane.

In 1988, in Rome, where I was enjoying the beneficence of the Prix de Rome, in the shock of discovering that my three years of Latin in junior high school and my perusing a basic Italian book on the way to Rome did not provide me, alas, with proficient Italian, which discovery by itself suggests I did not deserve the Prix—in short, while I was hiding in Rome from Italy, suddenly Texas, where I had spent the previous ten years in a kind of civilian Vietnam tour (roofing), came into focus. Texas's pride in itself, which reduces or inflates to pride in pride itself sometimes, suddenly became a manageable nostalgia. Strange emotions are to be had if you spend a year in a country you think full of people yelling at you under the duress of comprehending nothing they are yelling. Even country music suddenly sounded spectrally good; somehow I had a tape by the Trio (Dolly Parton, Emmylou Harris, and Linda Ronstadt, I think) that I played in the high-ceilinged artists' studios in the Academy, and it sounded like a music of the spheres with what may as well have been Odysseus's sirens singing it. I even envisioned for the first time getting some pointy-toe Lucheses, maybe even a hat. One morning, hungover (I was not hiding from Peroni), I composed myself and composed this:

> Yesterday a few things happened. Every day a few do. My dog beat up another dog. He does this when he can. It's his living, more or less, though I've never let him make money doing it. He could. Beating up other dogs is his thing. He means no harm by it, expects other dogs to beat him up—no anxiety about it. If anything makes him nervous, it's that he won't get a chance to beat up or be beaten up. He's healthy. I don't think I am.

That is a not inaccurate portrait of a boy a bit trembly from the circumstances I was in and of this dog that would come to compel me to write about him for twenty-two years. The speaker in the story is very loosely based on a small-time would-be dogfighter I had met in Texas whom I have already in flinging him into fictitude falsely ennobled with mental capacity. But the dog is my dog, a pit bull bought five years earlier in North Carolina but essentially a Texas dog, his sire bred thirty miles (Baytown) from where I was living

(Houston), his dam's main progenitors bred in San Antonio. For the cognoscenti, he was a heavy Carver dog by way
of Stinson (who bred Art) and Perry and Cummings. For
the skeptical who will drop the veil of Michael Vick discred-
itability in front of whatever honorable utterance I might
now come up with about the fighting dog, this dog was bred
as well as any professional fighting dog you could buy, or
steal, at that moment in the world. And that is why a sane
and unsentimental man is compelled to write about him for
twenty-two years even though the dog was not allowed to
fight professionally. This is tantamount to saying one had
a good racehorse bred in Kentucky of champion horses and
one loved the horse though he was never allowed to race.
The characteristics that would have made a splendid racing
horse made him a splendid non-racing horse. It is a finally
silly-looking argument, and I make it.

I waited another thirteen years before succumbing to
the urge to memorialize the dog some more, the dog then
dead seven years and my missing him only in its early fester.
In 2001 I wrote this about him for the *American Kennel Club
Gazette*, whose editorial diplomacy suggested that we call the
dog an Am Staff (American Staffordshire terrier, which unlike the generic pit bull the AKC recognizes) if it came up
(we didn't let it) and that we change, rather comically, the
word *fighting* to *confrontation*, and *fight* to *confront*:

> A dog is the only friend you can have in life
> who will go with you wherever you want
> to go, whenever you want to go, without

question and without putting on his pants. That is the quintessence of dog that secures our affection.

No questions, no pants, my dog, until he was killed at age 11 by a bobcat, was ready to go. He was capable of intimating that I was his first choice in traveling companion. No, that is inaccurate. You do not perceive in a dog the mechanism of choice, or preference, or judgment, or valuing one thing over another, and this is the second facet of the dog that wins us. He is coming with you because you are you. You? Let's go! With you, it's all good, he says, and you cannot help but love a thing that says that.

My dog would lead, get ahead by 50 feet, and select a fork in the trail and take it. If I paused at the fork, said, "Spode, this way," indicating the other fork, he would hustle back agreeably and take it. This was a complex, loveable moment: In it he said, Shucks! Alas, I presume! Goofy me! Shoulda known! You're right, boss! Better all around this way! And off he went down the path to the next fork, unabashedly presuming to pick a path there and repeat the little minuet of false humility if I again called him back. He'd do this all day, grinning.

My dog did not lie abed depressed. You

don't get depression from a dog. A dog doesn't do down. This is the third magical facet in the bright furry diamond that a dog is. He's ready if you are, he's not wearing any clothes, and he's not depressed, and what on earth is better than that?

Near the end, my dog did lie abed a bit longer when he heard a noise than he would have when young. He was 11, had no canines left, was partially paralyzed in the rear from weird coral-like ossifications on his lumbar vertebrae. So when the bobcat (if it was not an outright panther, which over time I have come to think it was) made its first unprovoked snarl just outside his house, he let it go. When the cat made a second horror-movie noise, it was too much. He got up, creaked out there, apparently engaged big cat with no teeth to engage it with, apparently got cut pretty badly, hiked about a third of a mile down some of our path forks to a place where fish die on our property after high water, bled copiously there on his good German-steel collar, was found there a week later with the help of buzzards, and had his bones recovered there six months later, which I bleached and have boxed in a Rubbermaid Roughneck. It was not the worst day of his life. There was not a finer moment than confrontation, and there was not a finer thing to confront than an impossibly large cat—almost his size or three times his size—and if the cat prevailed, well, to him, that was another occasion for the grinning aw-shucks shrugging off of dubious judgment, so what. His collar is still in the woods, corroded by the salt in his blood to an inflexible rusty mass reminiscent of an abandoned bicycle chain.

I recently was involved in the mercy killing of a bobcat struck by a car but not killed. When the game warden dispatched it with a neat, nearly invisible shot between the eyes, I took it to the taxidermist, paid $388.88, and now have it standing on two curious pieces of driftwood on my living-room floor approximately over Spode's old house under our house. The cat looks like an agreeable fellow himself, and I wish we could walk the trails together, the three of us, and delight in meaningless corrections of the way to go.

And now I am months away from sixty years old publishing a book (*You & Me*) in which mention of this dog is a *bona fide* recurring element. I am in the full fester. Spode is gone now eighteen years and I think of him almost daily. I have even made efforts to locate another dog. The breeder in North Carolina is not in dogs anymore and reports there is not a dog in North Carolina (he means the real deal; he located a hack breeder who was in the game way back and is still breeding trash). The breeder in Texas is out of the game but has a son in the game and I was offered a dog but I wanted a puppy not a two-year-old. I lost my nerve. I may get it back. I might be, in writing this, talking myself into driving to Texas. In a moment I will tell you why. But here for now, from *You & Me*, is the evolution of the Spode elegy today. The speakers are two unnamed men, one of whom is claiming to have owned my dog in the lovely Ça-n'est-pas-moi dodge that fiction is (that is, I am talking but it ain't me):

> My dog died. He never lost his enthusiasm for me. I now lament that I did not play with him more. It gave him supreme pleasure if I got down on the ground and he would turn me over to go at my face, insanely, insanely wagging happy. I should have spent all day doing this. It was a pure thing, he was unrestrainedly happy. I had the capacity to give something on earth that. There were days, weeks, I did not do this, I schlepped by leaving him alone.
>
> You were a turd, but he knew you were an okay turd, that is why he did the licking.
>
> My father sold his Parker shotgun out of our garage one Saturday morning for $20 instead of giving it to me. I was thirteen or

so. Why did he not give it to me? I would like to have gotten to the bottom of that, and to have talked to him and known him at the end. I schlepped right by all that too. But what I am saying is that I regret more not playing with my dog. I think in this preference I am displaying the trait or traits that put us where we are.

Without lives, men who are not neat and brave and Buster Brown *bustamente*, you mean.

We really are going to be afraid and we really are going to also refuse to die and we will give away the free dignity and purchase the other expensive dignity. I have known this since I could not even put my dog down. Fortunately he was eaten a little bit by a cougar.

That was a stroke of luck.

You are telling me.

The tail end of this was actually written in 2009, so I have written about a dog really for only twenty-one years. Not so bad. The full fester of sentimentality with an asterisk on it.

Here's the deal: dogs like this are not afraid of anything, and men afraid of things, as I am (of *everything*), take great solace and cheer from being just near that which is not afraid (and if that which is not afraid loves you, it will haunt

you the rest of your fearful life). This operates very openly
at the dog pit ("At one hour," a dogfighter will say, "I made
him cur out"), and it operates at the dog park too, or in the
boardroom, or in the Volvo, or at Starbucks.

I had a dog not afraid, it gave me great cheer and blustery
vicarious happiness. I am a coward now with no blanket.

New Orleans

New Orleans resembles Genoa or Marseilles, or Beirut or the Egyptian Alexandria more than it does New York. . . . The Mediterranean, Caribbean and Gulf of Mexico form a homogenous, though interrupted, sea.

I realized that New Orleans might be exotic in some respects but that in others it was exactly like everyplace else.

—A. J. Liebling, *The Earl of Louisiana*

I lived in the Quarter for two years but in the end I got tired of Birmingham businessmen smirking around Bourbon Street and the homosexuals and patio connoisseurs on Royal Street.   —Binx Bolling, in *The Moviegoer*

If I had to live in a city I think I would prefer New Orleans to any other—both Southern and Catholic and with indications that the Devil's existence is freely recognized.

—Flannery O'Connor, *The Habit of Being*

When I get to New Orleans's Le Richelieu Hotel, the single room I've reserved is unavailable and I've been upgraded, I learn, to a suite—the Paul McCartney Suite. "Someone must have detected I'm a writer," I tell the young desk clerk, Jack. "As a matter of fact, sir," Jack tells me, "it's highlighted right here on your reservation slip." Indeed it is. Jack goes on to instruct me in the particulars of the boon I've fallen into, some seventy dollars' worth of free bigger room, and sends me with a xeroxed flyer to Greco's Restaurant, where I can get a complimentary drink for having been referred by Le Richelieu. I don't know it yet, but already I'm in a kind of seeming accidental series of events that will not seem finally so altogether accidental, and it is a phenomenon that I will begin to think perhaps peculiar to this city. One deigns avoid the term *conspiracy*, after Oliver Stone took Jim Garrison to the movies, but there is in New Orleans an advanced sense that things small and large are *possible*, that oddments of time and place and people can conspire here to make things novel. For now, on the surface of things, Jack is taking very good care of a tourist, and that, too, is endemic in a city that entertains seven million tourists a year, a city whose French Quarter must be the largest, densest, least meretricious tourist attraction in the country.

It's late and Greco's is closed so I get from the French Market grocery on Decatur dinner, a six-pack of Dixie beer, and a quart of orange juice. They have the famous muffaletta there too, I notice. "You guys still making sandwiches?" I ask of the two proprietors, one of whom chuckles as the other says, "Forget it." It's said agreeably. As I leave the store, Forget It says, "Hey, man, you left your beer," indicating on the counter a sixteen-ounce clear cup nearly full of beer that is not mine. It belongs to a drunk young woman wearing a black bandeau and a black skirt and black tattoos with an abdomen-forward posture so intriguing that I watched her make her purchase as I waited to make mine. "It's not mine," I tell Forget It. "It's that . . . chick's who left." *Chick* has popped out of my mouth—not, given the context, inappropriately—for the first time in my life. Forget It is sufficiently Brooklynesque that I think he'll appreciate the term. I'd catch the chick and tell her the hoser in there's got her beer, but she's gone. Decatur Street is good for this aspect of New Orleans: it's not the pastel Land's End tourism you'll see in tonier parts of the Quarter. At its other end in four days I will see a black guy squatting on the sidewalk doing a spiel about how you must be somehow messed up to live in the Quarter. "You be a kook or weird or some kinda messed up *for sure*—hey, baby!" he says to a girl skirting around him—"watch me, baby, watch me—"

"I'm watching you," she says, with a kind of Dinah Shore self-advisory lordliness.

"—yeah, watch me, 'cause if you walking home asleep tonight, asleep on your feet, *I'll wake you up!* 'Cause I'm like a . . . like a *tree*."

She's not there to ask him how he's like a tree; she's in the constant stream of street-walking drinking oohing ahing tourists. Not far from the squatting tree, yet on rich Decatur, in the window of Sidney's grocery is a photograph of a naked woman so large she suggests a giant hairless shar-pei.

When men visiting New Orleans point this out to their women, their women say, "Oh, gross!" Small plastic obscene toys flank the shar-pei Heavy Date.

In the morning I ask why the suite I'm in—and it is a boon: from kitchenette to full-mirrored wall in the bedroom I pace off at close to forty-five feet, past porcelain cranes and Chinese armoire and two televisions—why the suite I'm in is the Paul McCartney Suite and am told by way of answer it's his, Paul's, fiftieth birthday today. In *The Times-Picayune* the first article to catch my eye is of Dewey Balfa's death at eighty-one. Balfa, the Cajun violinist, is credited in the notice with resurrecting Cajun music from "the mere chanky-chank" by Barry Jean Ancelet, who is perhaps the principal historian of that revival, and whom I met ten years before as an accidental chauffeur for musicians at the annual Cajun music festival in Lafayette that Balfa began and Ancelet was helping produce when I showed up as a driver. Elsewhere in the paper I note that Rockin' Dopsie, whose band performed at that festival, and my favorite chanky-chank band, will be at New Orleans's Maple Leaf Bar the following night. I make a note to call Barry Ancelet.

In the sports section is a photograph of the young man I rode in with on the airport shuttle. Nearby headlines about a disgruntled Carl Lewis suggest the photo is of Carl Lewis, but it's not. It's of my unheard-of sprinter from Raleigh, or Durham, who is one of thirty-one runners qualified to compete against Lewis for an Olympic-team berth in two days in New Orleans's track and field qualifying trials.

The twilight-zoney warbling of odd conjunctions in New Orleans is obtaining.

It is easy to make light of my thesis of the Enhanced Possible, inviting even to discredit oneself before others do. I shall not mention the matter overtly again, I hope. The idea may be spurious, is certainly corny, yet is tenable, finally tenacious. If you ask a woman who lives in Atlanta and visits New Orleans on weekends what she likes about it, she will say, "The atmosphere." "What about it?" "It's . . . seductive." She means, you think, *open*. "The sense of history," she adds. She can't articulate the matter any better, or worse, than you can.

At the Old Coffee Pot Restaurant, where I've gone for breakfast, judging my quart of orange juice inadequate in a place with as many restaurants and as many good restaurants as New Orleans has—certainly one cause for the feeling that New Orleans is our most European city—I want gumbo instead of world-famous rice cakes or eggs, and the waitress checks with the kitchen. The gumbo's ready but the rice not. I am allowed my gumbo neat. I will try gumbo until I have gumboitis in the next four days and this is the best. My waitress, when I ask for a paper menu to take, calls an office somewhere trying to locate one and has a man move a cash register looking for one before finally pressing on me one of the sixteen-by-twenty-inch laminated tri-folds that I protest won't go in a suitcase. "Fold it," she says. What I wanted was this: "The Old Coffee Pot Restaurant has long been a favorite of the native New Orleanian. You will find many colorful local folk dining here because of our truly Creole cuisine as well as the quaint and relaxed atmosphere. Besides catering to our city friends, we find it a joy to serve the many visitors from all parts of the world. You may have dined at the Old Coffee Pot and not have known you were dining with Royalty...." I noticed no Royalty, but did watch a heavy, perspiring man with a parboiled, burst-vein complexion in a fine white shirt and elastic-waisted blue seersucker pants have coffee with another heavy man not unlike him—colorful local folk. The claim of serving not *just* tourists is not uncommon in the Quarter and not untrue, and it is one reason the Quarter is no more meretricious than it is. At some eighty city blocks of clubs and joints and restaurants and shops and music bars and sports bars and gay bars the Quarter must be the largest block party in the world, and were there not an indigenous, permanent citizenry keeping it honest, as it were, it would be abysmal. But the Quarter is three stories of Creole architecture, and the block party is on the first floor. Above it are people living their lives, as exotic and plain as Mr. Liebling would have them. They live in and around the twenty-four-hour hustle below, and it is they—hardly accessible to the visitor—who keep the visitor in some kind of awe of the place, I think.

Fifteen years before my current visit, I met in Pass Christian, Mississippi, a couple who had recently come home from Europe to settle in these rarefied top two floors of the Quarter and be, as nearly everything about it suggests one be if settling there, artists—she, whom I misremembered as Josephine Sabacco, to be a photographer, and he, whom I correctly remembered as Dalt Wonk, to be a writer. I want to see how they fared—and get myself off the first floor— but have difficulty phrasing the call, knowing they won't remember me.

If getting above the block party is difficult, getting away from it is too. My first escape, inspired partly by the hope of locating the freely recognized existence of Miss O'Connor's Devil, is to jail. Specifically, to a prison called Jackson Barracks, where I'm invited to witness a class in lexicography. Specifically, the inmates are formulating a dictionary of jailhouse slang specific to Jackson Barracks under the direction of a professor of English I met in Turkey. That he taught many years in Beirut is not beyond the coincidental.

The one term certifiably specific to Jackson Barracks is a name for itself connoting its relatively easy conditions: Camp La-La. Indeed, the inmates have come in wearing flip-flops and we have coffee and cake. They enjoy making the dictionary. We spend considerable time on a curious term, *hot eyeing*. It means, roughly, to spy on another inmate for personal gain with the Man. It has been advanced that one might be doing something at four in the morning and someone might hot eye you. One cannot ask in jail what folk are in for, but I hazard to ask what one does, once in, at four in the morning. "Well, for example," an inmate says, "I might go get my boy for some sex and this dude pretending to be reading is really hot eyeing me." The group nods in approval of the definition. "Can I take creative writing at the University of Florida?" the inmate with the definition at this point asks me. "Sure," I say, not sure how he knows I teach it or *that* we teach it at Florida. "How do you know so much about the University of Florida?" "I'm from Orlando." Orlando is eighty miles from where I teach. The Devil is in the room, I'm sure, but he doesn't seem altogether evil. A little frisky, perhaps. At the end of class we shake hands all around, firm look-you-in-the-eye handshakes, and I leave Camp La-La wishing for a class of college students as articulate and attentive as the prisoners of New Orleans.

"That New Awlins is a *pahtying* town," a man told me once, with his leg up on the bumper of his car and a dreamy, appreciative gleam in his eye. We are in a park somewhere in Louisiana during a summer of indiscriminate rambling around the South on my part, and the swarthy fellow waxing fond of New Orleans is Cajun, a new species of human to me. He's not wrong about New Orleans. Here's a New Orleans party night:

Eat well at R&O's Restaurant following brush with Devil at Camp La-La, R&O's a big, festive, folksy, fried place you can buy your four local hosts and yourself dinner and drinks for $71.91 including 15 percent tip which is not enough, once outside look across Lake Pontchartrain at Covington where Walker Percy made Binx Bolling and despaired of getting through ordinary Thursday afternoons and at Mandeville where they shanghaied Earl Long and where "going to Mandeville" means going nuts, and go downtown to a bar

named Phoenix where you've heard they wrap a naked man
in Saran wrap but all you see there is a cage and some man-
acles and a noose and underwear on rafters, stop at a place
called the Rawhide because the number of cars suggests
something going on but it's not the entertaining New Meat
Night it's just rather plodding strippers who look like Hec-
tor "Macho" Camacho, so catch Walter "Wolfman" Washington out at Tipitina's who looks like Jimmy Walker, plays
like James Brown, until he bites his guitar and the Hendrix
fix is in, he's wearing polyester or rayon or some kind of
clothes so shiny you can't tell if they're wet but his face is,
he's playing his heart out and getting real good when the
show's over and you're outside standing around wondering
where to go when the Ringling Bros. and Barnum & Bailey
Circus trundles by in trucks and some of you feel like joining it and some of you feel you have, you go to Benny's Bar
where what the newspaper calls "soulful acid-blues quartet"
Irene and the Mikes is playing and Irene is a dead ringer
for Janis Joplin if Janis Joplin had had a smooth sweet voice
and *Vogue* cover-girl looks but she didn't but Irene does and
you lose a little of your tourist reserve and tell a fellow at the
bar "At heart Irene is Janis Joplin" and he tells you "At heart
Irene is *Irene*" and on that beat Irene goes into Janis Joplin's
"Down on Me" and you leer at your adversary without any
tourist reserve and ask a woman you can't tell if she's with
this big fat guy or not to dance and she says no thanks so you
ask a guy who's certainly with another woman who really
can dance if you could dance with her. We see outside a guy
climbing up on his car, not the hood but the roof, to crash;

now the fat guy is in full-throated sing-along with Irene and a guy dressed like a minor pro golfer is touching a railing like it's a woman he's dancing with and Irene *passes out drumsticks to everyone in the bar* and you and everyone start whacking all the surfaces in the bar in and out of rhythm and outside the guy on his car is snoring and there's a just palpable concern for his safety among you all who have survived another club and are at modest loose ends not knowing whether to go home while the going's good or not, admit defeat and go somewhere else; at Fat Harry's they won't let us eat at two or so but we can play some kind of laser pinball you lose 4,000,000 to 24,000,000, billiards at another place where I demand tonic water and watch my friend team up with the spitting image of an unironic Martin Mull, much funnier than ironic Martin Mull, and beat some local boys who take their pool seriously enough to call all their shots to *me* because Martin Mull doesn't know what they're saying and my friend, winning, doesn't care what they say or do, but he wants to eat upon the theory that cholesterol damage will reduce alcohol damage so we're in the Clover Grill back in the Quarter ordering breakfast at 4:21 and the waiter, a guy named Rose, hot eyes a boy at the counter who's come in without a shirt and Rose tells him "It's not *me* it's the rules of the City of New Orleans" that prohibit his being served shirtless, and Rose offers to make him something to go and the boy goes out, hitches up his pants, shoots Rose a big finger but Rose is taking orders from three men in a booth one of whom slaps him in the butt and then squeezes it making the ordering a rather social event and my friend is waiting to leave, I get to bed, bed, bed I hope not to wake up for a very, very, very long time; on this day Paul McCartney turned fifty and Dewey Balfa died I know how they feel. New Orleans is a pahtying town.

Drinking, alas, is something that also figures in the European feel of New Orleans. Bars do not open improbably late nor close impossibly early for the serious drinker— which is to say, more to the point, that New Orleans is not clouded by the arcane and non-secular blue laws that plague the rest of the country.

Alive, my friend—Kyle Brooks, an architect currently in New York—and I go to the house of an old friend of his, a painter named Emery Clark. The house is a consummate restoration in the Garden District, and to let us in Emery Clark has to stop us with sign language from touching the door and fiddle with her alarm system to disarm it long enough to let us in. The process is noted and Emery Clark tells us of her husband's watching a man break into, in broad daylight, the house across the street. It's bad enough, she says, that she wants to leave. I will later hear of other people in neighborhoods recently gentrified who are now giving it up. One account involves calling a security service to meet you at your car and escort you into your house.

Emery Clark and Kyle Brooks do their catching up with each other and I look at her paintings. Some photographs of her children catch my eye. They are stylized, strikingly composed black and whites. They are signed "Josephine Sacabo." I have found my Josephine Sabacco.

I call and arrange to meet Josephine Sacabo. I go down to A Gallery for Fine Photography on Royal Street on the chance that Ms. Sacabo's book, *Une Femme Habitée*, is there. It is. So are the plates of the book and new work from Nicaragua. The pictures suggest to me precisely that above-the-block-party essence one can intuit here, and manage in their haunting mastery of chiaroscuro to suggest, if not freely recognize, Miss O'Connor's Devil.

I meet Ms. Sacabo and Dalt Wonk at Croissant d'Or, a tile-floored serious coffee place for natives in the Quarter. They are perhaps more amazed that I remember them than I am at finding them and finding them together and finding that they've done what they were setting out to do fifteen years ago. They've gone to New Orleans to be artists, and they're not in a Tennessee Williams play. Their recall of our meeting is vaguer than mine, and our reunion is appropriately awkward, but it is not as uncomfortable as it might be—New Orleans can render the improbable possible, as I relentlessly maintain. Josephine Sacabo confesses she has partied too hard the night before and takes her leave, graciously—New Orleans is a pahtying town, as I relentlesssly maintain. Dalt Wonk and I walk about a bit, he showing me things about the Quarter above the first floor. "Let's exchange coordinates, as the French say," he proposes, and we exchange addresses.

Checking out at Le Richelieu, I pay my respects to Jack the desk clerk. He tells me he was studying writing at Tulane but quit and now wants to go to Hattiesburg and study under

Frederick Barthelme. The one school to which I applied and was accepted at other than the one I went to was Tulane, and I studied writing under the late Donald Barthelme. I wish Jack the very best of luck.

Bermuda

Going to Bermuda with a banjo on my knee. Going to Bermuda with a banjo on my knee. Supposed to go to Alabama with a banjo on one's knee. Bermuda is better than Alabama for the banjo knee-going, sweet home or no. I know about the sweet home, I went to school with 'em boys what became Lynyrd Skynyrd, I knew Allen Collins, the skinny girl-beautiful guitarist, I put Allen Collins in every travel piece I do, travel writing is harrowing, going to Bermuda with a banjo on my knee.

Travel writing is harrowing. You go where the Travel Authorities assume people should generally want to go and you are charged with making people generally want to go there. You are in paradise, more or less, having to prove it is paradise. It is hard to have a good time trying to figure out a way to say you are having a good time, whether you are having it or not, even in paradise. Allen Collins's arms were not bigger than the neck of his guitar when I first saw him play it. We were fourteen. He played, I watched him. He became a millionaire rock star by the time I was a straight-A sophomore in college paying a third share of $55 rent. Then Allen died. I limped on. In travel writing you do not mention jail, plane crash, or acknowledge writing per se. I have just violated these tenets. I feel better. I hope the Travel Authorities allow it. Travel writing is also harrowing because you have to ping the nodes of the code of the genre while of course convincing yourself that you are soaring openly or secretly above the genre. The harrowing in its several aspects will make you daft. As I have, I think, amply demonstrated. Let's move on. Let's do Bermuda in Moments, with subjunctive Points of Advice.

A Moment in History

Bermuda was slow in colonization. People couldn't find it, it was so low, and when they did find it it was usually the hard way, foundering on reefs that ring the islands (the Bermudas, 181 islands, defined as anything two feet above mean high water large enough to support life) for miles out. It was not on the way home from the New World, outside the prevailing westerly winds. When people wrecked on the reefs they spent five months, three months, a year rebuilding their ships or building new ships. Then they got away. Hogs were put on the islands, deliberately and as victims also of shipwreck, providing eventually a handy maritime pork store. The first money coined on Bermuda after it finally did get some colony action going had pictures of hogs engraved on every piece and was called hog money, according to Mrs. Mary Gray, who has written the shortest and, until I saw Rosemary Jones's *Bermuda: Five Centuries*, my favorite history of Bermuda. The first known black man on Bermuda was called Venturilla. In 1744 the governor was named Alured Popple. I credit Allen

Collins with having had the wit to come up with Lynyrd Skynyrd to make fun of Leonard Skinner.

A Moment in Geography

Bermuda was also difficult of access because it was not in the Caribbean with the other islands. "The Bermudas" sounds exactly like "the Bahamas," but it's not. Even the library classifies Bermuda in the Caribbean section, which will be found as a subset of the Latin American suprasection. I was paying $18.33/mo. rent and Allen and the One Percent, as I'd known them, were opening for the Who. It was hard to believe. Bermuda is not even tropical. The charm of the tropics—the heat, the chaos—is not there. If you dragged Barbados 1,364 miles north toward Greenwich, Connecticut, or if you dragged Haiti 1,035 miles north, and replaced the mad French influence there with the civil British footprint (the same civil footprint in Kenya and India), you'd have Bermuda. Another way to make Bermuda would be to collide Greenwich, Connecticut, with Barbados in the Large Hadron Collider in Geneva, Switzerland. Either way, dragging or colliding, same result. The hot sauce the color of yellow road paint made from Scotch bonnet peppers in the corked bottle in Barbados that will remove yellow road paint from a road if applied for that purpose and that you store with the cleaning supplies under the sink when you get it home and that no one will put on food is not to be found in Bermuda. In Bermuda the hot sauce is red and it is Tabasco, or Frank's, or Trappey's, or faux Cajun stuff from New Orleans, and it is all made in New Jersey or New

Orleans, and has a screw cap. You can see a chicken fight in Jamaica and you can see two feral chickens on a golf course in Bermuda, or one feral chicken on a fancy hotel lawn.

I waited a tad too long to do my profile of Allen Collins because when I finally worked up the gumption to call him, in 2000, I discovered he had been dead nine years, owing to complications of his paralysis, which I knew about, having met the son of the surgeon who fixed him up after that last car wreck, but I did not know that it had all finally ganged up on him and killed him. I did not know that. Allen was very sweet. I knew that.

A Moment in the Wawer

In the Wawer, Bermuda, handily straight across from Fripp Island, South Carolina, was a good base for running fast sleek cedar ships through the Union blockade of the Confederacy. They took British gun parts in, took cotton out, the trade carefully laundered by a Confederate consul in Bermuda to keep Britain clean, according to a Reliable Anonymous Source you will meet in due time. Hold your horses. This puts me in a good frame of mind as I set foot on the island. What is better, finally, than the Hopeless Old Fond Lost Cause, as foolish as it was, and a civil island in the middle of nowhere where maybe just like a minie ball on our ground you might dig up a piece of hog money on theirs?

A Moment in a Taxi

My driver Sean Simons is seventh-generation Bermudian and he tells me that cruise ships put 5,000 to 7,000 tourists a week on the ground in Bermuda in high season, that 65,000 or 67,000 permanent residents ("They did a census but never got a dependable number") handle them as hoteliers or restaurateurs or taxi drivers or tour agents but some of these residents are not concerned with touring, they work for the "exempt companies," and Hurricane Fabian in 2003 wrecked a lot of chicken coops, hence the "wild chickens." If they get in your yard you can either keep them or call the authorities who will remove them. The exempt companies constitute the large industry of "reinsurance," the business of insuring insurance companies. The big new buildings downtown are invariably the houses for reinsurance, and the law offices and accountancy offices that attend the business of reinsuring the insuring. The business is reputed now larger than tourism and is also called "offshore finance."

A Moment in Paradise

At my hotel, a grand yellow affair called Elbow Beach, paradise strikes, as it will. I am told they've been waiting for me. I ask the doorman and porters at the door to allow me take my own bag to my cottage, one of ninety-five on the fifty-acre grounds, and they do, reluctantly, given my assurances that I can read the Where's Waldo map on my own and find my way downhill in the dark to Alamanda, among Bougainvillea, Caprice, Frangipani, Poinciana, Sea Grape, Easter Lily, Poinsettia, Gardenia, Oleander, Jasmine, and Honeysuckle, the multiple-unit cottages. In my room I am overwhelmed by three strawberries dressed in black-and-white chocolate tuxedos. Moreover these cute little fruity gentlemen are riding on the back of a swan drawn in chocolate on the platter reminiscent of Picasso's bull scroodles on his plates. I want to call my Companion and tell her what she is missing. One is supposed to have a Companion in these ventures so you can report what your Companion has for dinner when you have something else and so forth. But I have left Compania at home where she wanted to walk her dog instead of come to Bermuda and now I want to tell her what she's missing. I go to the beach and get a hamburger that runs $20 but I stay on keel with that because I am hungry, they manage rare, it's Black Angus—but the cheap gene has had a feather ruffled, at the least. Back at the room the cheap gene has all its feathers ruffled when I discover that Wi-Fi is to cost me $13.95 or $31.95 or $77.65 depending upon whether I am a one-day or three-day or seven-day fat cat. How do you charge someone $500 for a room and please him with the courteousness of the doormen and delight him with strawberries and then nickel-and-dime his ass into a Marxist rage? I glance at the door-hangy breakfast menu. The Elbow Breakfast is $31.50 per person, so skipping down to A la Carte I see Freshly Squeezed Juices, orange or grapefruit, $10. *I can't take it.* Choice of Two Eggs, $14. *No!* This offends the common man. I am the common man. Should the common man not fight the Man? When I reach this state, the phrase that dominates my brain is *rich fuckers.*

I walk up to the lobby, where I have convinced myself I can use the internet for free. I pass through a stupendous ligustrum forest I can hardly appreciate now that I am a soldier in the Revolution. There I discover of course that the internet usury continues. I play myself in a game of billiards on a table that does not require coins, *mirabile dictu*, while watching a BBC story on the recent shooting of a black kid in Orlando by a Hispanic security guard named Zimmerman. *Seven dollars an egg!* Where I come from an egg a la carte is fifty cents or a quarter.

A Moment on the Beach

On Elbow Beach, three generations of women from Baltimore are asked to distinguish Bermuda from the other islands:

The grandmother, who has been to fifteen-odd islands all over the West Indies, from St. Kitts to St. Lucia, thinks.

The mother says, "Cleaner . . . quieter . . . safer."

The grandmother agrees.

The mother says, "The others are wilder. On Nevis you can go to a sugar plantation, but you are on . . . high alert."

The grandmother agrees.

The mother and the grandmother agree that on Bermuda you are on no alert.

The girl, four or five or six, keeps her opinions in these matters to herself. That there is no sugar-plantation-going on Bermuda does not concern her. Yet sound of body and sane, she wants to get off the beach and go see Daddy.

A Moment Downtown, First Points of Advice

Coral, teal, pink, navy, lime, wine, tan, yellow, white, gray, khaki, light blue, gold, green, black, Madras plaids, and Breton red are some of the colors the eponymous shorts come in, and poly/wool, poly/cotton, poly/linen, and Madras cotton are the fabrics they come in, and the place to get them is the English Sports Shop, where I would advise you to, and I did, go and get some. Helpful British gentlemen will help you. They fitted John Lennon for a custom-made suit shortly before he was killed. Did he get the suit? Mr. Creamer says it was posted to him, and Mr. Hamshere says that his manager (Mr. Creamer: "His PA, personal assistant—" Mr. Hamshere: "Yes, what was his name?" "Seaman." "Unfortunate name—but it has an *a* in it") came down and said they might bury him in it, so he is sure John Lennon got the suit. John Lennon spent a lot of his last two years on the island and a memorial to him is planned. He sat for a portrait by the painter Nancy Gosnell in Mr. Hamshere's wing chair.

The Bermuda short chiefly differs from the casual short in the matter of "rise," the difference between the outseam and the inseam. As the waist increases in the Bermuda short, the inseam shortens (a 10.5-inch inseam in the size 38 casual short would be a 9-inch inseam on the Bermuda short, e.g.), effecting, in Mr. Hamshere's decorous phrasing, "more ballroom." I ask Mr. Hamshere if he is familiar with the tape of Lyndon Johnson's ordering Haggar slacks and requesting the crotch be let out lest they "cut [his] nuts" and feel like "[he's] riding a fence wire" but while he is most sympathetic to Mr. Johnson's plight he is not familiar with our presidential history to this extent. The inseam of the Bermuda short falls behind the outseam when looked at from the side of the leg; thus the seams are not parallel as they are in the casual short. The inseam-side hem in the Bermuda short is cut to rise about a half inch as it approaches the inseam, describing a shallow triangle; thus the inside hem is a half-inch higher than the outside hem. This higher hem inside the leg prevents the fabric in there from flapping. You do not want flappy on the inside of your leg wearing the Bermuda short. That might be a worse affair than want of ballroom owing to inadequate rise. With these critical features of the Bermuda short in place, you can get ten pair or twenty or thirty, and match them with thirty pair of knee socks, and wear these to work every day of the year though the winter is sometimes not deemed shorts weather, and be natty beyond natty. A man in a proper pair of these shorts is a proper man.

Beneath and behind the English Sports Shop in an old livery tunnel made now into a shopping arcade is the Gem Cellar run by Chett Trott. There are Trotts all over the low country of South Carolina. Possibly the Trotts of South Carolina are some part Bermudian. Bemudians went to South Carolina, among other places, in the early days seeking better religious propositions. Chett Trott has made a pair of hog-penny cufflinks in 14-karat gold that I want very much for my new shorts outfit but they are $715 and I don't get them. But this is decidedly where I would get them. The nice silver Bermudian toad for $55 is more my thing. I don't get that either. I've got ballroom and nothing flapping inside my leg and I'm good.

A Moment Back o' Town

Back o' Town is the area in the north of Hamilton reputed to be where the "shooting incidents" are happening. There are not many of these but, for a place alleged as few as fifteen years ago to not have a gun on the island, shooting incidents are bothersome. The incidents are gang-on-gang. Gangism shows American influence. Rose Jones says, "You know the saying, when America sneezes Bermuda catches a cold?" Ballistics are suggesting that one gun has been used in several shootings, and even that the same gun has been used by both gangs. The conclusion is that while it is true Bermuda no longer has no guns, maybe it has just one gun.

In suburban Back o' Town is a sandwich takeout place called Art Mels. It is white in decor, black in clientele, doing heavy business at two in the afternoon. Rockking, son of Art and Mel, runs the counter. The fish sandwich runs $10.50, can come on wheat or raisin bread, with slaw and with hot sauce they make on premises that Rockking is proud of. The fish sandwich weighs about two pounds, about a pound and a half of which is fish. A person should not eat one entire in a sitting, but he probably will. An elderly fellow in a Kangol cap comes in and says to the Filipina helping Rockking, "Heya, darlin."

A Moment in Earnest

I rehearse my qualms about travel writing in front of my Reliable Anonymous Source, who is not unfamiliar with the practice of it himself. I do the subtle soaring-above-the-genre to his delight. He's pretended that himself, it's clear. "You marshal a set of misimpressions into an amalgam of misapprehension that makes everyone mad," I say (he nods gleefully), "and then you pretend in two days to have understood a place—"

"I wouldn't get it right myself," he says. "It's worth a brief think. A brief one, because there isn't anything underneath.

And if there was it wouldn't be anything interesting." At this he laughs the laugh of the inveterately irreverent, the laugh of people who like to quote Oscar Wilde. Which he next does: "Your hotel is the hotel that dare not speak its name." "Bermuda should send a delegation to Orlando and ask Disney to take it over." "You mean, like a theme park?" "Yes!"

The laugh that accompanies these sentiments is the one where you put your knees tightly together and pump them up and down, your fists pounding them a little to help with the pumping up and down, and the pumping seems to help the tears come out of your eyes. It is the silliness that goes beyond the silly into the true that you are after in these fits. Silly liberates the vision for the sincerely insincere.

The Reliable Anonymous Source is a sincere wooden-boat enthusiast and I ask what he knows about the fast cedar boats that ran contraband to the South. "They were *fast!*" he says, suddenly not joking. "They were ballasted with cut stone from here and it was allegedly used in the foundations of homes in Charleston." He sent a writer once to Charleston to develop these allegations. There was also talk of some plastering or stuccoing that used Bermudian elements in Charleston successfully in ways that the elements had never been so successfully used in Bermuda. The writer never filed the piece. C'est la vie.

"When Cuba comes online," RAS says, meaning to the American market, "that will be the final nail in the coffin of Bermuda."

He is convinced that Bermuda loses traffic to the islands to the south because they promise sunshine in the winter.

"If a couple in New England wants to come, at least one of them will insist there's a greater likelihood of sunny weather in Bahama." He thinks Bermuda has to market itself as a year-round destination, not just a summer joint. Indeed *The Royal Gazette*, the island paper, that very day runs a feature in what it calls its "Tourism in Crisis Series," "'Guest Comes First' Policy Pays Off."

There is some talk of my being put in touch with the expert on Bermudian stone and Charleston ways with Bermudian pink sand, if that's what it was, the secret intelligence never filed, but I prefer to let it remain the secret intelligence never filed.

A Moment Eating

I would go, and I did go, to the Black Horse Tavern way up-island on St. David's Island and talk to Judy, the main hand, and Gary Lamb, proprietor. Gary Lamb is old Bermudian, the recipes at work in the Tavern are eighty years old and from his great-grandfather, he fishes, he builds, he has an accent that will get away from you and that would be familiar to anyone who's been on Johns or James or Wadmalaw Island in South Carolina, he is weathered, the whole effect is reminiscent of Robert Shaw as Quint in *Jaws*, the rheumy eye, burnt skin, solidity all shouting what people must call a Character. There is no pretension. If he says he'll git y'shark fer ye, he will get your shark for you. He has seen people on Bermuda make money and change and it frankly chaps his ass.

"Is there a roux in this?" I am speaking of the fish chowder that has been set before me and that is good.

"No," Gary Lamb says.

"What makes it this dark?"

"Burnt flour."

"That's a roux."

"Oh."

Gary Lamb clearly knows how to take a roux down to the Hershey's-syrup stage, longhand for burnt flour, but not that it is called a roux, and he doesn't care. This is a fine gumbo with the elements reduced smaller than you do in gumbo. This is the best gumbo I have had I did not make. Maybe it is as good as the stuff Barry Ancelet made that night in Scott, Louisiana, that made us stop drinking Jameson after drinking it all day and eat the gumbo and not die.

They put fried wahoo in front of me that is the best fried fish I have had. They put half a Bermudian lobster with a stuffing that has sugar and a herb I cannot identify in it that Gary Lamb won't identify. I eat it. The Bermudian lobster is a little tougher than the Maine or Florida lobster, rather gratifying. Gary Lamb tells me he served some mullet roe to a principal in Watergate whose name eludes him who said, "This is the best caviar I have ever had," and Gary Lamb asked him if he was fleeing from Watergate, and he said no.

The mullet roe must be carefully cut from the fish so that the sacs are not hurt and so that the yoke joining the two lobes at the front of the fish is intact. The lobes are rubbed with salt until they begin to sweat and feel cold, fifteen to twenty minutes. Then you put a paper towel on the counter and a piece of wax paper on the towel and the roe on the wax paper and another piece of wax paper on the roe and a piece of plywood on the whole deal and weight the plywood, or you can clamp the roe between two pieces of plywood and screw down the clamps but put a half-inch spacer at the top and bottom of your press so you do not go too far and crush the roe. After a day of this pressing hang the roe in the sun for four or five days and do not let it get wet or damp or mildew will ensue. The finished roe will be hard, like a biscuit, and is eaten like a biscuit, the British biscuit. Some people even put it in their lip like skoal. Once Gary Lamb found some roe in a drawer that had been there four years and he ate it and it was good. If I were to eat at one place on Bermuda, the Black Horse Tavern is where I would do it. I would in fact stay on this down-scale end of the island. Across the water is the original capital, St. George, as quiet and seventeenth-century quaint as sunny Bretagne.

A Moment in Transcendance

Nadia Aguiar and Tim Hasselbring, young citizens of Bermuda, take me onto the roof of the aquarium at the Bermuda Aquarium, Museum and Zoo. Tim Hasselbring drives the boat for the aquarium and has had the cured roe and says it is like slicing hard Parmesan or Romano cheese. We squat down next to the open-air top of the North Rock Exhibit, which Rosemary Jones in her Moon handbook to Bermuda calls "the first living coral-reef exhibit of its scale in the world." Nearby is a trough on an axis dumping water into the tank at a regular period to simulate surf forces that the coral below need. Nadia pats the water and Tim tells her to pat it closer to the edge. "Don't lean out like that." I see a barracuda, a big one. "That's Spike." Up wells a darker, thicker, heavier fish. He is coming toward the hand patting the water. He is a grouper about four feet long the size of a large dog and he comes to the hand to be petted like a dog.

It's my turn. I take Tim at his word and do not lean out and I pat the water at the very edge of the pool. The fish edges toward my hand. His name is Darth Vader. I estimate him to be closer to a hundred and twenty pounds than to eighty but I know nothing. I pet him, stroke him slowly, avoid the eye the size of a half-dollar, as dark and sober as a plum, as it slowly develops what this is all about: Darth Vader would like us to find some parasites and get them off his ass. I totally want to be a good boy to the big boy. He raises his gill plate. Gill plates can cut like a razor. But that is when a fish is fighting you. This fish is asking you to do a fellow a favor. I reach under there and feel for leeches, more afraid of touching the gills themselves, and there is something called a gill raker that they kill fish with I do not want entering my consciousness but it has. I am transported. This is something that would thrill a boy to death and it is almost making me a boy again to do it and I am fifty-nine-and-eleven-twelfths-years-how-did-this-happen-to-me old. I stroke him lower down. "Can I have sex with him?" "No," Nadia says. "Okay." I am changed by this, as different a person as we can be made different by small large things that happen to us. This outfit is a serious conservator doing serious conservatoring (Harvard and NYU are involved) and I am coming back here, when I come back, to see my man Darth.

A Moment in Color

Candy pink, primrose yellow, banana-pudding yellow, *yellow* yellow, white, green, blue, new white, beige, ivory, turquoise, old white, brown, chartreuse, red, and eggplant are the colors of the houses up and down the islands, driving which takes about an hour, and all the roofs are white white. There are dozens or hundreds of bays and beaches, some most quaint and protected and private-feeling, all easy of access. And in them you face why you would want to come to an island like this: the water. The water cannot be captured by a camera or by a boob saying it's incredible. Its colors juxtapose in bands that move, functions of depth and wind and shade that change, a psychedelic palette of plain old blue blue, chalky cornflower blue, glass cobalt, tincture of iodine, Granny Smith and chlorine, sapphire, anole green, diamonds, mercury beads, potassium permanganate, Waterford crystal. Edge it all up with the stunning cool white of refined sugar or with the cinnamon coquina. Sit there and look at it. Pop the polarized lenses up, down, up, down. Arsenical green shifts to indigo, indigo shifts to arsenical green. You can do it all day.

Gumbo

About thirty-five years ago, 1980ish, I was sitting one night in a kitchen in Scott, Louisiana, at a fake redwood picnic table on a fake redwood bench after a day of driving a van hauling musicians to and fro Barry Ancelet's Festival de Musique Acadienne et Créole and we had been drinking beer all day and had moved to Jameson and it was maybe about eleven p.m., we'd passed Dan Jenkins's Stage 5 Fuck Dinner at I would guess about six or seven, when Barry Ancelet, the dean of all things Cajun and a person of some quiet authority, said, "Let's have a gumbo!" and as I gathered he meant food I thought he'd lost his mind. He strode to the stove and cooked something and then from a chest freezer beside the stove got out some bricks of something frozen and as I continued to ply the whiskey and think he'd lost it he put the bricks of something in the pot with the other something and a neutron wave hit me, some gaseous sublimation of greenness and grease, that arrested the march into oblivion completely. It reversed time and space to somewhere before Stage 5 Fuck Dinner, and it said I *was* going to eat something—all I had to do was find out what it was and get it out of that pot. And I had found—owing to this Cajun dean's lunacy, his deciding that falling-down drunk we would eat—one of my foods.

[Forty years later Barry Ancelet writes me, "If you use the gumbo piece, please correct the part about the table being made of cheap redwood. It's important to Caroline, especially. It is in fact made of old sinker cypress that has a reddish golden hue, and was handmade by a furniture maker named David Broussard, who also made several other pieces in our house, including the china cabinet, the armoire, and the dictionary stand (all of the same sinker cypress). . . . We have never owned a chest freezer. Ever. (My parents had one and I learned then that they are a pain in the ass to get things out of.) And I have never put frozen vegetables (onions, etc.) in a roux. Ever. Would not work. Too much water content. Too cold. Might even explode. The eastern-most edge of our table is very nearly due north of the stove, and it runs east–west along the wall—eight feet long—with cypress/hide-bottom chairs along the south side and on the two ends and a cypress bench along the north side (along the wall). It has been this way for roughly 39 years. I swear to God." He is correcting me about the geographical position of the table I got so wrong because I had told him I thought it northwest of the stove. My point here is that I had these details horribly all wrong, to a hallucinatory degree that I think is beyond the false memory induced by booze alone. I submit that the extraordinary wrongness is attributable to the hallucinatory power of that first good gumbo on top of the booze. No other explanation for this degree of en-feeblement on my part is to hand. I plead gumbo.]

•

A man, unless he is a Frenchman, has only a couple of foods that command his attention. That he will read about, track down, travel for, presume to criticize others for liking poor executions of, etc. And that he will learn to make. We all have these, often to egregious effect, but sometimes not. I found out what gumbo is and have made it for thirty-five years. I can make it better than any commercial instance of it I have had except at Cochon in New Orleans by that chef whose name eludes because he did not answer my message when I wanted to profile him. I hope he is still alive because many of the people I have wanted to profile and haven't have died on me: in alphabetical order Bob Burns, original drummer for Lynyrd Skynyrd, ran car into tree; Allen Collins, original guitarist with Lynyrd Skynyrd, complications from paralysis from running car into I know not what; Blackie Collins, knife designer, Gerber LST, ran motorcycle into what I do not know; M. C. Davis, largest land conservator in the southeast United States, ran into Stage 4 lung cancer. I am not going any deeper into the alphabet and am not wanting to profile anyone at this point. I've killed enough as it is.

I made gumbo once to entertain at a friend's house on Bourbon Street, and Slim, the houseman, who at first refused to have any of the gumbo, did finally assent to have some and said, eating his second bowl, "I'm shocked, you being from Florida and all." Another time I put tomato in a seafood gumbo against counsel and ruined it. Gumbo is not a foolproof food. Care and very careful carelessness must be taken.

A *Gumbo*

Bones and vegetable scraps for making stock

Meat

(Andouille) sausage

Roux

Celery

Peppers

Onions

Okra

Tomatoes

Parsley

I am going to say here some things that might accelerate you into grasping gumbo. Do some reading: look at the *Joy*, of course, then read Paul Prudhomme as your real primer. Look at his pictures of roux making. See the one where the roux looks like Hershey's Syrup. That is what you want. One is supposed to use a light roux with a dark meat, but I like to snort at this. There are not many dark meats anyway. Raccoon is a dark meat, but not many people are going to be making raccoon gumbo (they should). Withal, make the roux *dark*. Take time making it dark—not fast.

You may take thirty minutes or more toasting the roux. Do not feel that your life is wasting away, just wonder as you sweat over this stuff, constantly stirring it, what, say, Putin is doing at this very moment, if he has his shirt off on a horse and is cool. What became of Yeltsin?

The vegetables that go into stopping the roux will be rendered invisible. Only those added later will be present—okra, typically, but not in every gumbo, and green-onion tops, sometimes tomatoes that you want to see and feel. Both the invisible and the visible vegetables can be off-list. The on-list is celery, peppers, and onions, annoyingly insistently called the Trinity. I have used celeriac, leeks, weird peppers, eggplant, heavy parsley. I'd use a beet but the purple scares me a bit. Fresh peas would disappear very nicely in stopping a roux. Find what you have and have at it.

Use rich stock; make it yourself from every bone and vegetable scrap in the house. For seafood stock get big heads and backbones. Since you will have spent a fortune on the seafood your fish man will give you all the head and carcass you want.

Brown your meats in the oil you will use to cook the roux. Typically you want two meats (in seafood gumbo, several, though see below when I say goodbye). One meat can be thought of as an "accent" meat; it is commonly a cured meat or otherwise exotic compared to the main meat, and you use less of it. Sausage (the Cajuns call for andouille sausage but they do not mean true andouille, though if you can get actual andouille you should) is the most common accent meat. Squirrel is a good accent meat. Squirrel can be the main meat. A squirrel gumbo can be insanely good. A squirrel tastes as good as the animal is athletic and smart. If they were not as athletic and smart as they are, they would not require extermination for the problems they cause, such as penetrating the attic and making alterations to the electrical scheme that are not up to code. But athletic and smart they are, and uncertified as electricians etc., so sometimes you find yourself with a supply of them for accent meat, or main meat, in gumbo. God had this Life Path more or less in mind for them, insofar as He is All-Seeing, but I do not think Darwin had the path in mind.

I was stumbling along on my Life Path one night when I went into a second-story bar in Matagorda, Texas. Most likely this was before 1980, so it predates my experience with Barry Ancelet's undoing Dan Jenkins and the natural order of the universe. It was a Thursday night and Thursday night this bar offered free food. The free food was in a pot. It looked like Coca-Cola. If you dug around in the Coke with a ladle you brought up whole half crabs, without legs. White heavy crab chunks in shell. The liquor looking like Coke did not taste like Coke. It tasted good. Extremely good, and it infused the crab meat that you sucked out of the recesses of the shells from those plasticky compartments separating crab muscles. I suppose they are chitinous dividers. This crab was so good that you hollowed out the shells completely, then got more of the false-Coke liquor. This was the best free food I have ever had in a bar. It would be the best food I have ever paid for in a bar had I paid for it. It was gumbo but I did not know that. The word did not cross the threshold until Barry Ancelet said it. But this nonetheless was it.

Okay, you are set. If you read a little and work at it, you and your Path will be changed and you will have proper gumbo. The chef at Cochon is Donald Link. I do not want to profile or kill him. I will certify his gumbo if you want to start there.

Squirrel

Sometimes I have to stop in a grocery store—I like a country IGA—and get me the small handsome bottle of Goya extra-virgin olive oil, I don't know why. Sometimes I have to go out in the yard and shoot the squirrels, I know why. Once a squirrel poked his face out of the hole he'd eaten in my Rubbermaid garbage-can lid to get the chicken feed inside the garbage can, before Walmart ruined Rubbermaid, don't watch the *Frontline* on that or you will be *incensed*, and I at last deployed some of the no-pain-no-gain martial-arts skills I have sweated into myself tearing the medial meniscus in my knee and rupturing the radial sagital band on my middle knuckle right hand and so forth, by popping the squirrel back into the garbage can with a hammer fist. I then induced him to leave the hole he'd eaten and took aim with my pistol loaded with .22-long rat-shot shells, but he froze, with genius, behind my chicken waterer, a $150 industrial appliance that a squirrel knows a man is reluctant to shoot through. No matter how bad the man wants to shoot the son of a bitch eating his irreplaceable Rubbermaid feed bins and his feed, the son of a bitch eating the cans and the feed knows the man won't shoot. He calculates his next move, and when he makes it, the man will humiliate himself one way or another, shooting the waterer after all, or shooting the roof of the coop, shooting his own foot, or hand, or face, or dog. He will not shoot the squirrel.

His humiliation will grow along these lines until he supplements the .22 with the 28-gauge Ruger shotgun with the handsome slender English stock, a gun as elegant as an egret, and begins, ever so incrementally, to reduce the humiliation by pushing squirrel through the one-way membrane unto Death.

Optional: Sharpen you a basketball-inflating needle and insert it into your squirrel once he's on the Other Side and inflate him to the size of a cane toad, robbing him of dignity. But let's be clear about something: this is a majestic creature, superior to your athleticism and to your wits on your feet, and if you make him look like a toad and a little blood spittles out of his orifices when you apply the air, that is really no derogation or detraction from the glory of this animal at all, so now proceed.

Not optional: Squirrel fur is parfumey and sheddy. A good small hunting knife, such as those you might get from Wayne Hendrix in Allendale, South Carolina, or Bob Dozier in Springdale, Arkansas, is contraindicated. Get you some good scissors and insert a sharp tip into the skin—if you have cane-toaded the squirrel the skin will be loosened—at where the waist would be were the squirrel wearing a shirt and pants, and cut this waist around him, or her (look later for fetuses), and then with good old-fashioned slip-joint pliers get a grip on the shirt and a grip on the pants and remove them just as you would the shirt and pants from a tiny child. Skinning is done. I have saved you a lot of homespun down-home old-boy perorating, and I have spared you the quaint unworkable instructions in the otherwise eminently sane and dependable *Joy of Cooking*, complete with its Gorey-like cartoon of boot on squirrel tail on the ground. Tail on ground don't work in the hands of the neophyte. Shirt and pants do. This will take thirty seconds, though budget considerably more time in cleaning the corpse because while the cleaning proper is quick you may slip up and start to marvel at things that will throw you into the *God v. Darwin v. neither* debate if you are prone to it, such as the fetuses, or the huge and finely veined cloisonné testicles that look like a big, pretty delicious-looking bean or nutmeg in cross-section, or the impossible deltoid muscle extending from navel to shoulder that accounts for this animal's unequaled humiliating vertical climbing acceleration and power. A squirrel is a *man*! It is a tiny robust *bear*! Extract the little musk or scent glands allegedly in the small of the back and under this deltoid muscle in the armpit (where it is hard to locate a defined gland but there is discolored-fat-looking stuff, get it out). Now we ready.

Your naked tiny child will look like a skinned puppy, which will give you pause, or not. Puppies are probably delicious.

These *faux* puppies certainly are. I spare us the tacky calling of them "tree rats" etc. Grant us relief. Cut into anatomical units that make sense and that can be browned evenly (if you can accept uneven browning, or want to use a lot of oil, leave the puppy whole), season with salt and pepper, brown them up. If you have been hunting diligently and have a lot of squirrel in the freezer, I find that sixteen squirrel has a kind of natural-law feel to it, like a peck or a furlong or a pound.

Put them aside, on a plate where you can look at them and consider eating them in this state, very tenable if you have taken them past light browning and if you can do tough (not that tough, try them). Into the pot put copious onion and parsley, I like prodigious parsley, it is rendered invisible anyway. Put the squirrel back in, add some stock to braising level, cover this dish, ought to be a Dutch-oveny kind of unit, put in oven under 300 for two hours or so. Go outside in yard with or without gun and get any chanterelles might be out there, or some other mushrooms won't kill you, put them in with squirrel at end.

Cook some rice. I hope you have a proper steamer but almost certainly you do not. Edwin Poulnot III in Charleston who used to sell them to me as the last gasp of Kerrison's Department Store has stopped answering his phone and I am afraid may have passed on. A friend in New Orleans, when I shamed him for making such a huge to-do about rice-eating in Louisiana without his having a proper steamer, found some nice steel ones at the Crystal Rice Plantation of Crowley, Louisiana, called Blue Rose Stainless Rice Cooker. Lay these squirrels that have been responsible for so much humiliation and God's or Darwin's or neither's glory over some of the rice with mushrooms you have found or not and see if they are not really good.

Let's say you do not like the idea of whole pieces of rodent on rice: okay, fair enough. Bone the braised squirrels and put the meat into a Brunswick stew such as James Villas's in his *Stews, Bogs & Burgoos*; it's an aggressive recipe with bacon and a ham hock and okra in it. Or use the squirrel in a gumbo, I'd go with Paul Prudhomme on the gumbo because Villas has the inane idea that a gumbo roux should never be dark; use the squirrel for the chicken in Prudhomme's chicken-and-andouille gumbo. In either the stew or the gumbo use the squirrel-braising liquid, which will be nuclear heavy, as stock. I sometimes never open my Goya oil bottles, so handsome and well shaped, little golden statues, and it's always good to have some fresh oil on standby, just in case, as the Russians say.

William Trevor

By threatening to write a profile of them, I have killed two people named Collins. One was Allen Collins, a tenable target since I went to school with him and knew what little nothings we were, coming from nowhere, with nothing, in Jacksonville, Florida, westside, more nothing than southside, before Allen became a rock star.

We do not have the time to detail the second Collins I killed with intent to profile but he is Blackie Collins and he designed a piece of cutlery you have had in your hand or a knife or tool that his brilliant designs made someone else copy. Motorcycle crash three or so years after I talked to him laying ground for a profile. He designed the Gerber LST and I had the rare red one in my pocket when I stepped up to him at a knife show and he told me he designed it for Gerber asking for a Corvette as fee and credit in the catalogue and they gave him the Corvette, which by weird coincidence in the killing-Collinses scheme of things he picked up in Jacksonville, Florida, but they did not give him the credit in the catalogue for the design, a truly revolutionary industrial design moment, and that angered Blackie Collins and he became an expert witness against Gerber in

Tim Leatherman's lawsuit for Gerber's stealing his designs
for the first multi-tool, and Gerber lost the case, and there
we were all set to do a profile that I knew I uniquely could
do and Blackie, like Allen, went and died on me.

I have cooled my jets on targeting folk to profile them,
as I think anyone might understand given how I wiped out
the Collinses, and when Ann Kjellberg asked me to review
William Trevor's last book of stories (unless his estate goes
Hemingway on us) I said Yes meaning No because I do not
think a book review serves a man or a woman or a book, as a
kind of corollary tentacle from the navel of Pierre Bayard's
notion that even reading a book does not serve a man or a
woman or a book, a tentacle that will safely carry you across
the waterfall of this nonsense, a conceit I take not from
Carlos Castaneda's first book but from a subsequent book,
do not waste your time on the first book, which I assigned
the last class I taught in a thirty-four-year schoolmarm career that went well until that last class, which derailed, I like
to think, because the navel tentacle is not in the Castaneda
book I assigned thinking it a good example of the novel as
fraud. *All* novels are frauds, I tried to aver, insofar as they
presume to suspend a more or less gullible person's disbelief
(I could not uniquely profile Coleridge, but no more Cs even
if he is conveniently killed by someone else) for hundreds of
pages of usually not well written prose or what have you. I
said Yes meaning No, no review, I will do a little profile of
Trevor, which I uniquely can do, for two reasons: first, I cannot kill him because he has already conveniently went and
died—have you noticed that the past participle in English

is on the way out, perhaps at a rate faster than those of the objective case of pronouns and subject-verb agreement and grasp of the restrictive modifier? Have you noticed that English, if the interweb continues unabated, and nobody going to abate it, in fifty years will be inutile? Where are we? I have lost even myself. Not good. Focus. Bob Dylan's getting the dynamite money killed William Trevor, not out of outraged pique or sourness, and I suspect he was charmed by Mr. Dylan's putting ice fishing over podium slurring, but at a point Mr. Trevor, who, however modest, and I sense he was consummately modest, not unlike Peter Taylor, his American counterpart, whom I knew not well enough to uniquely profile but well enough to know that his consummate modesty was perhaps the one aspect of his character smaller than the delight he took in the naughty—however modest he was, Mr. Trevor knew he was dynamite-money-qualified and ninety, and he saw Dylan invited but not going to Stockholm, and he said, Ah, that's it then, and died. It may have not killed him but it kills me. (It occurs to me that Mr. Trevor in his passing may have predated Mr. Dylan's getting the dynamite money but this does not of course alter my arguing that his getting it killed them who do not get it whether the demising, the not getting, is after or before the getting.)

Second (good luck tracking that, just proceed), in the thirty-four-year career of schoolmarming, successful until it derailed at the end (I had a little Woody Hayes because students weren't writing and pronounced the course over four weeks before it could be over, and five of nine students never returned; the four staying and I then had the best class in my thirty-four years), of teaching that which cannot be taught (the writing of fiction), I taught almost exclusively the stories of William Trevor. *The Collected Stories* is pound for pound the most literary bang for the buck in the English world. Let's skip the blurbist review Pablum—"By turns funny and profound," "Trevor is astutely perceptive of human truths"—you think? The book is the most telling demonstration of how to write (and why to write, if we want to get into the unteachable Pablum for real) there is. Trevor is a formalist, by which I do not mean what one is supposed to mean by the term (which meaning I think I knew once, in the acuity of the dead-serious sophomore trying to fund his intellectual fundament), if its meaning inheres in something some Russians said in the '30s and over here Brooks and Warren and a third fellow were heavily on about, a William Empman–ish? (Why don't I just interweb it and get his name? Because I won't.) By formalist I mean that if there are fifty stories by William Trevor in front of you, there are fifty different robustly executed forms of narrative before you. The impulse to write a story different in structure from his last seems to have been the first thing on Trevor's mind, as heretical as that may sound. I have not been custodial of appearing to be sane here, why start now. I am submitting that Trevor is so good a writer that he can sit down to do an exercise in form and prevail upon whatever debate-lowering restriction that frivolity might impose and write right over the obstacle and pull it off.

Time signature: "Virgins" will be in present tense and

98 percent of it will have happened in the past, narrated in past tense, demonstrating (for the American student who will ignore) the proper restriction of present tense. "The Day We Got Drunk on Cake" will be 98 percent in the dramatic present, told properly in the past tense, as superficially light as the title suggests, and break your heart and frighten you for the depth of the hero's "prevailing condition of emotional delicacy," a phrase tendered in the opening paragraph that you ignored for its flippancy.

Presenting the problem: Trevor always establishes the problem immediately, sometimes overtly, top-down ("Without meaning to, Verity had taken her mother's place"), and sometimes covertly, in accreting details that I think demonstrate what was called "inductive logic" in those sophomore courses where I attended so hard and futilely to my intellectual fundament. Two stories below will detail the inductive problem.

Point of view: In "On the Zattere," Verity Unwill (above) is aware she has without meaning to taken her mother's place, and in the next paragraph her father is also aware she has done this and likes it. They will be seen together at the end, Mr. Unwill penultimate, Verity ultimate, delivering in its structure the close two-person story that Trevor intimates in the opening. In "The News from Ireland" Trevor will enter of the heads of hero, hero's sister, hero's object of affection, hero's object of affection's object of affection, hero's antagonist, hero's antagonist's wife, and hero's antagonist's children, stopping just short of entering the heads of the hero's antagonist's children's pets, demonstrating how many POV one may have (infinite) and the concept of the diminishing return as it pertains to points of view in the domain of romantic fiction, as Twain liked to put it.

In "Access to the Children" Trevor uses three-fifths of a point of view for the hero (the infamous unreliable narrator, one here two-fifths impaired by booze and denial and by the debilitation of divorce and its denial), a narrative restriction that requires Trevor to break a Big Rule (Twain: "There are nineteen rules governing literary art in domain of romantic fiction—some say twenty-two") to add a late, minor POV for the duration of one observation that delivers information concealed from us by the two-fifths' impairment of hero. The hero's wearing a green tweed suit in need of pressing and jangling his keys—seedy and happy-go-lucky at once—is in the opening sentence. In the opening two paragraphs of "Lunch in Winter" Nancy Simpson seems to have been married four times, and we see her interest in young tennis players and chaps in the Bayou hotel lounge where she likes to stay, as she puts on her face to meet yet another man for lunch, one whom, we learn in another couple paragraphs, she was married to long ago. We get the idea, inductive logic, that Nancy Simpson may be what they once called promiscuous. Is this term used today? Nancy, it will develop, at a time when she was not married to Simpson but to a fertilizer salesman in Philadelphia, conceived one of her children not with the fertilizer salesman but with the sunken-chested (tubercular) boy whom she found playing the rear half of a vaudeville mule. Are we right? May we say promiscuous? Trevor has Nancy, fully unimpaired, *tell* us (another Big Rule he likes to break [since it, Show Don't Tell, is the singularly largest piece of hogwash in all the Rules]): she believes in Mr. Robin Right, and if she just keeps looking, with all five fifths of her wit, she will find him. Mr. Robin Right, in fact, if she remains courageous, she tells us "will come bob, bob, bobbing along." She is one of Trevor's heroes ruined and saved by *indissoluble belief,* all the more supportable in his view for that belief's putative insupportability. She's the kind he likes, the naughty who will be naughty for those of us afraid to be, like the best of naughty vicariousness in his American counterpart Peter Taylor.

Other heroes are wrecked by loneliness that subsumes them (living in Romantic Westerns, marrying known thieves, to not be alone). Others by social pressures (a boy's being consummately cruel to his mother, whom he *knows* he loves beyond anyone else, because she is a social embarrassment). One social pressure, not to be deemed senile lest one be sent away, forces an old lady to allow her house to be wrecked by delinquent teenagers sent there to paint it, in the course of which they have sex in her bed and release her budgerigar—the man who engineers this "social service" I want to hunt down and kill every time I read this story. I will kill also the husband of the woman whose baby Mrs. Lacy adopted and must now give back according to the advocacy of this new husband. Look—I'm overlong in this thing and at the point where I am admitting I want to physically harm fictive perps. It is time to wrap up. I have not husbanded sanity deliberately here but this has crossed a line. As we

Democrats like to say, solving all our problems, this is unacceptable. Betty Lacy is four and just last week made a mess of the groceries by trying to make a cake. Brigit Lacy will give her up. I can't take it. Trevor can make you fight people who do not exist. That is writing. Dynamite-money writing if there is any of it at all.

The book Ann Kjellberg wants me to review came in the mail two days ago; it is on the captain's desk ten feet from me in its US Postage Paid, \$2.66, Media Mail–stamped brown Jiffy mailer. (The desk survived Hurricane Irma because we took it to the second story.) The book came by book post and this magazine is called *Book Post*, maybe the inaugural post (propitious precedent? I'd think not). I am not about to open the book. I am told it is called *Last Stories*, and it's Random House. I can't wait to open it, but I can. As long as it is there, the stories cannot be read, yet, but there they are. This is like Christmas. Let's savor it. These stories are it, unless, as I say, they Hemingway Mr. Trevor. I will read the book slowly, a page a day, maybe slower. This is it.

ps/

I broke down and read this book. I read it slowly and desultorily, knowing that these are the last stories of their kind on earth. They are as noble and precious as the last dead elephants will soon be. Trevor came to the end acting like it: these stories are bleak. They are simpler than the earlier stories and operate on one or two narrative planes where once three or five narrative planes operated. They sometimes are a tad looser in the time signature, a ridiculous term I use to mean chronological order, our knowing crisply when is when. If when is when is a bit looser here it may be because when is the end. It is getting dark and Trevor sees things through to the end. People do some dying here, they get down to basic last wants and memories. Lifetimes of longings circle back around to long-last fruition, and the fruit is not bright fresh fruit. Gird yourself. Trevor is brave, brave, and strong, a phrase I heard a man say of himself once at a mall.

Peter Taylor

I knew Peter Taylor a little. On this irrelevance I am going to recommend the new Peter Taylor Library of America volumes to you, strongly. With the force of even stronger irrelevance I stand ready to recommend virtually any LOA volume. Not as irrelevantly as it might appear: my house flooded last year. Six cases of (my own, remaindered—an author must buy his own books when no one else will and they are only $.75) books I forgot about under a bed absorbed enough Hurricane Irma water to explode the boxes and promote the fat, slimy books' sliding about the room, almost like liquid themselves. These two hundred books became a pile of heavy slimed paper it took canoes to carry to shore and a tractor to carry to a burn pile itself the size of the beautiful orange tractor. I saved the other three hundred or so books in my house. Among them are six Library of America volumes. If all the other books had gone the way of the burn pile except these LOAs I would feel, all in all, fairly okay about it. I'd miss the Signet Classic *The Rose Tattoo* and *Streetcar* paperbacks printed in 1956 and now too delicate to even touch, and the two *Three by Flannery O'Connor* bound now in duct tape. A Tennessee Williams paperback already the color and texture of a moth's wing dissolved by tannic floodwater with snakes in it would make a man weep, one who is already on the edge because the snake swimming by the kitchen sink was not a snake but a lesser siren. But if the three hundred books had also gone to the burn pile, by then the size of two tractors, they'd never have had to be handled again; the goddamned library could handle one's need for books, and I could have sat tight in my moldy uncluttered house with just my six gorgeous and good-to-the-hand Library of America volumes. I have the memoirs of Sherman, the only 1,136-page book I have, and will ever have, read; *Grant* at an even more improbable 1,199; *O'Connor, Collected Works*; *Faulkner, Novels 1930–1935*; *Crime Novels, American Noir of the 1930s & 40s*; and a volume of Roth, at one time the only living author published by these visionary people. I cannot tell you the volume of Roth because it is with the daughter I bought it for; the *Crime Novels* is also for a daughter but apparently I took it back. Girls need in my view to know about crime and writing about crime and they need to read a Biggee who can in a sentence or two show a person how to write. With these books in hand—bound in a cloth so fine and palpable and real that "cloth-bound" is not alas a mystery; printed on paper so onion-skinny that it confers a scriptural authority to the text; written by people who invariably *can write* (to borrow an endearing sentiment from the anti-abortion front, the LOA don't make no trash)—I could have made it, waiting for the slimy book pile to get dry enough to burn. And now the Library of America has added Peter Taylor, possibly more obscure than anyone yet on their august list. It commands attention.

•

Peter Taylor is the kind of writer one discovers by overhear-
ing better-known writers talk about writers. When one is
young, say, and poking about the gods, the demi-gods can be
glimpsed in the woodwork. Often these demi-gods are what
gets called writers' writers, the most damning of faint-praise
damning. One learns from Flannery O'Connor that Robert
Fitzgerald and Peter Taylor have recommended her to John
Crowe Ransom for a Kenyon Review Fellowship; Robert
Lowell tells her that he has visited Peter Taylor at Kenyon.
Explaining the influences upon a writer of whom Evelyn
Waugh would say "If these stories are in fact the work of a
young lady, they are indeed remarkable," O'Connor reports,
"I read the best Southern writers like Faulkner and the
Tates, K. A. Porter, Eudora Welty and Peter Taylor . . ." It
is likely that one can know the names of Robert Fitzgerald,
John Crowe Ransom, Robert Lowell, and all the writers
preceding him in her list of Southern influences, possibly
to include knowing that "the Tates" are Allen Tate and
Caroline Gordon, without yet knowing this name Peter
Taylor, last—in *prominent* last place. This is how, roughly,
unless you were around for Taylor's heyday publishing in
The New Yorker in the fifties, you might come to know where
Peter Taylor is on the radar (i.e., in what Pierre Bayard calls
"the collective library"). And now here he is, hugely, in 2018,
in the Library of America.

I met Peter Taylor when Donald Barthelme, who was dropping the bomb on the fledgling writing program at the

University of Houston that a writing program might should concern its students, not its self-important teachers (a position embraced with aristocratic conviction by those teachers), invited me to introduce Taylor when he came to town to read. I agreed to the job provided he, Don Barthelme, would review my introduction to prevent my committing stupitude. In assenting to this request for parental supervision he gave me an instruction preventive to stupitude: "Three-quarters of a page, double-spaced." I read Taylor, I read Taylor reviewers, I absorbed all the tropes used to talk about him, and Don Barthelme approved my introduction by excising one word: "miniaturist," which word I had used obligatorily because nine of ten reviews of Taylor at the time used it. "We don't like being called miniaturists," Don Barthelme said. We chuckled. Of course we don't, I thought. And Don B is linking himself favorably to Peter Taylor—another set of coordinates for the Taylor radar.

Before I broke the mold with the introduction, I rent another part of the adults-only fabric by going to dinner preceding the reading. At a big table full of adults I was sat a chair away from Mr. Taylor, a good purchase from which to study him. He was aged and Southern-courtly, just as he was supposed to be. I became distracted by a powerfully bad odor. Already nervous, I went into a set of speculations that made me more nervous. Perhaps adults, or at least these self-important literary ones, stopped bathing when they achieved eminence. Refined Peter Taylor clearly was not a man who would not bathe, but the gothic lurks in the aged Southern-courtly. A large operatic poet fairly nearby, with heavy arm fat, might not bathe. I leaned toward her, away. No change in the pestilence. I leaned this way and that, no longer listening to the false hilarity chortling all about the table. The smell was outrageous, pathological if it was issuing from a living being. I was waving to and fro like a bird dog or Ray Charles when I saw on the table in front of me a blond kaaba of cheese. No. Yes. Thank God. It was not the adults, and even the adults would not touch the cheese. The rest of the evening went without psychological disorder except that Peter Taylor read a story, "The Gift of the Prodigal," in which nothing much happens and nothing surprises or saddens or alarms or frightens or forces uptake of breath or a new awareness or a profound pall or, really, anything at all, nothing at all seems to go down, no serving up of the inimitable, no pinging of the unforgettable, no evanescent precious ambiguosity, and kind, smooth Mr. Taylor, who thank God does not smell like that cheese, is wrapping up non-demonstratively, non-remonstratively, unpreciously, just reading and stopping reading without your even having sensed the End was to hand, he has stopped, and you are crying. Because you are an *ad hoc* VIP and sitting in the front row and not in the back row where you'd otherwise be, you have to conceal these insistent weird tears. Something happened that no one saw happening. You have been in the presence of a Biggee.

I became what writer I could so that I would not have to talk about writing or listen to others talk about writing. I was successful in dodging the acquisition of these critical skills (though it is true that in becoming a schoolmarm I learned to talk about writing, if not precisely in ways that might be called literary criticism or even review criticism; in schoolmarming what we do is ask how might this writing be different so that it is not this bad next time). I tender this bio-news now for those reading this and anticipating my reviewing the book under review. I will speak, briefly, about *the writing* in a moment. I have to arrange myself a bit.

The actor Roy Scheider called Peter Taylor and offered him use of his properties in Key West and Manhattan. He did this, one was led to believe, because he thought Taylor good. Let's say he said something like this: "You're a hell of a writer and under-recognized, man, and I want you to have these places if you need them." Taylor would have said something like, "I don't believe in this kind of thing, but in this case I am going to make an exception. Thank you." (When the NEA called Peter Taylor to tell him he had won a $50,000 lifetime achievement award, Taylor told the NEA that he did not believe in the NEA but in this case he was going to make an exception.) Peter Taylor took Roy Scheider up on his offer of places to stay and work.

Don Barthelme brought Peter Taylor to his class in Houston. A student's story was read aloud on which we would comment. The story was a dialogue between unnamed parties. It was not a narrative-heavy thing but the kind of thing in which one can see or sense what I saw someone (Alfred Kazin? No.) call in Beckett "the wreckage of a narrative." In this wreckage a garter snake had swallowed a Christmas bauble, a fairly shocking moment in the to and fro of the dialogue. Then the dialogue ended without ending. It was hip. It was what Don Barthelme called "wacky mode." Don Barthelme said to Peter Taylor, "Peter, what you think?" Peter Taylor said, "Well, I'm just an old character-and-action man, so . . ." and he chuckled just a bit and made a gesture with his hand in the air that might be described as a hand describing a rolling motion. The chuckle combined with what he had said and with what he did with his hand to express his apology that he would be unable to help in discussing the story's merits, and it was clear that he would say nothing else. The discretion this showed, the high diplomacy, confirmed that Peter Taylor would never not bathe and never ask "What's that smell?" at table. Don Barthelme moved on to us to get the damning and wounding criticism. I marveled at how smoothly Peter Taylor had gotten out of it. With a model of the consummately polite in front of us we were free to be impolite. Biggees are *smart*. I wrote it down.

On a walk from the American Academy of Arts and Letters to a cocktail party at William Gaddis's, we (Peter Taylor, Donald Barthelme, and wives) stopped in at Roy Scheider's apartment in, I believe, a Rockefeller Building, or *the* Rockefeller Building, or maybe not a building with a famous name on it. The apartment was paneled entirely in heavy rich walnut. I have seen the Pasha's royal chambers in Istanbul and the Tsar's in St. Petersburg and never have I seen anything as sumptuous as the wood in Roy Scheider's apartment. The bathroom was done in glass three-quarters of an inch thick that held an aquamarine depth that looked alive. We were freshening up and freshening drinks. I'd won a modest prize via the benevolence of Biggees. It does not get literarily Bigger than it got at Gaddis's.

I came to know Peter Taylor better later when he moved to the town where I was schoolmarming. It is here that I can finally say something about who he was as a writer, and what he wrote. I asked him once if he could recommend one book to a young writer, what book would it be, and he said, without hesitation, "Turgenev." I asked him why and he said, "The envelopes . . . that keep going," and he made the same rolling gesture with his hand I had seen ten or so years earlier in Houston. On one occasion his son Ross and Ross's wife and their infant child were visiting. They were staying in the detached guesthouse and using a baby monitor when the baby was in the guesthouse alone. "When they go to bed they forget to turn the monitor off," Peter Taylor reported, and laughed. "Eleanor calls them to turn it off but I want them to turn it UP!" And he laughed again, a boyish unguarded happy laugh, from a man old enough that moments before as he got up from the sofa he had said, "What they don't tell you about getting old is that *your feet hurt*."

I have daftly peripatetted about in all this irrelevance now for pages in the hope of sneaking up on relevance. This does not always work, and one may appear merely daft. But here we are: this moment contains for me the essence of Peter Taylor and why he captivates and why he is major. Life is a surface of propriety with an undertoad of the naughty under it. Taylor and the better of his heroes live tortured proper perfect lives and long for the naughty. In this respect

Taylor is the American counterpart to William Trevor, who also brandished smooth well-reasoned social and narrative surfaces with outright kinky business slouching under the surf. Here are two passages from two stories of Taylor: 1. "I am listening gratefully to all he will tell me about himself, about any life that is not my own." 2. "[H]er behavior was such that it made me understand for the first time that this was not merely the story of that purplish-black, kinky-headed Jesse's ruined life. It is the story of my aunt's pathetically unruined life, and my uncle's too, and even my own. I mean to say that at this moment I understood that Jesse's outside activities had been not only *his*, but *ours* too. My uncle Andrew, with his double or triple standard—whichever it was—had most certainly forced Jesse's destruction upon him, and Aunt Margaret had made the complete destruction possible and desirable to him with her censorious words and looks. But they did it because they had to, because they were so dissatisfied with the pale *un*ruin of their own lives. They did it because something would not let them ruin their own lives as they wanted and felt a need to do—as I have often felt a need to do, myself. As who does not sometimes feel a need to do?"

The second passage is written twenty-two years earlier than the first. Jesse is a ruined black man. The first passage, twenty-two years later, concerns the narrator's wanting to hear of the "scrapes and jams" of his own white son. It is approximately the line that made me have to clandestinely cry in the theater in Houston after I had introduced Peter Taylor without looking stupid.

I framed a reading list for a course in forms of fiction with Turgenev at the beginning and Peter Taylor at the end. In between them were writers largely guilty of mostly wacky mode—the smooth run-on hysteria of Thomas Bernhard, the metastasis of Flann O'Brien's *At Swim-Two-Birds*, limpid-amber-prose-over-narrative-wreckage Beckett, Kleist's surreal real "Michael Kolhaus," best-of-all-possible-worlds *Jacques le Fataliste*, Grace Paley's mundane surreal, and so forth. I did this list without significant alteration for twenty-five years or more, and for twenty-five years or more students testified that it was Peter Taylor they most enjoyed, Peter Taylor they wanted to write like. I never understood it, I understood it. An old character-and-action man who delivers these narrative envelopes that keep going, who does no Look, Mom, no handlebars! ever, who is quietly, or not so quietly, unhappy with being happy, and who does not want to impress with ambiguity. The Library of America has done a solid. A serious literary person could live with one book if it were this book. Your house would have more room and a cleaner feel.

Saving the Indigo

How I Became a Fool for the Indigo

James Gregory's father, we were told, was stabbed twenty-seven times in a shell parking lot outside a liquor store in Jacksonville where, possibly, he worked. We never talked to James Gregory about it. We did not know James Gregory well. We put on a play in which we surgically removed a tumor from a patient using backlit projection on a bed sheet to better show the ghastly tumor lifted from the patient. The tumor was a live six-foot snake that in the projection must have looked fifteen feet long. We got the gasp from the audience that we wanted. I like to think that the patient was James Gregory, and that yada yada we were exorcizing a demon from him, but in fact I do not know that the patient was James Gregory and doubt that it was James Gregory since we did not know him well and I do not even often think of James Gregory in this or any other context. I do remember that after the show the snake was enjoying his stardom until too many children touched and grabbed at him and it became a kind of rock-star-fandom event that needed security and there was no security and the snake having had enough decided he was his own security and he bit Mike

Wilkerson on the thumb, and Mike Wilkerson shook him off his thumb and in that jostle we dropped the snake, who crawled under a long leaning stack of metal chairs for surcease from his admirers.

And let us pause. Were I to succumb to memoiritis, more frightening than Ebola, we might stop to ponder some things: What kind of place is this that children do not ask one of their own if his father really met his bloody end on a parking lot of oyster shells? This play—did I write it, making it my first literary production? Did it have pre-precocious Becketty repartee before the sockdolager of the fifteen-foot snake aloft frightens the entire theater? Could I not mention that I did ultimately do a good enough snippet of bad Tennessee Williams to stick it into my second novel and to be pleased with it even if virtually no one was pleased with the novel itself? Where might I stop? I might not, and that is why memoiritis is more frightening than Ebola.

We have a large snake under a long stack of leaning, heavy chairs. I am an agile twelve-year-old boy with a good sense of physics, which is what confers agility. The snake is under my charge. The snake has been put in my charge by my fifth-grade teacher, Shirley Brown. She has it because she has friends at the Jacksonville Zoo reptile house, whence it comes to her on loan. The snake will not be declared federally protected until 1978, but already in 1964 it is a rare animal. I have been allowed access to him to put him in the play. I am in charge and the snake has survived a fan event without security and is now under a ton of metal that can with less jostling than dropped him to the floor make those chairs slide, shearing, crash, and in my agile twelve-year-old brain cut him to pieces or merely crush him to one multiply bolused piece. The prudent thing to have done would have been to put my foot on the rubber foot of the leading leaning chair to secure the stack and ask Mike Wilkerson to get the snake, or, if Mike Wilkerson had had enough of the snake, to have him replace my foot with his and get the snake myself.

Maybe prudence had been abdicated when we decided to pull a snake tumor out of a person on stage. I got down and into the chairs and maybe Mike did too, and we got the snake out without incident; he did not, that is to say, bite us in the face, which we were presenting to him perfectly had he wanted to. I already knew that the character of this snake was special, having handled him some before his stage debut (I posed with him outside the Jax Zoo reptile house), but I suspect his agreeable demeanor at this juncture may have spoken to me in my "condition of emotional delicacy," which I borrow from William Trevor and will explain. The snake had no more quarrel with Mike Wilkerson's thumb. We got him into a secure cage and I had a nervous breakdown. Maybe that overstates it. The phrase "burst into tears" understates it. Let's say I was wracked by a sobbing that made it hard for me to breathe, or see much, but the little I could see included Shirley Brown's collapsing faith in me as her protégé. (She had called me this when introducing me to a man at a drugstore who was not her husband, whom I knew and liked, for his Hoss Cartwright mein and affect, and my adult-behavior alarm had gone off.) In my sniff-heaving I could not begin to explain to anyone the vision of those chairs, the hair trigger those old beige rubber feet were, what *one rung* of chair could do to a snake let alone five hundred . . . and I watched Shirley Brown dismiss me, and thought something like, Well, this is of course regrettable, but she has *no idea*, hail fellow and well met with her drugstore dandies.

For fifty years I have thought only occasionally about James Gregory (he was handsome), sturdy Mike Wilkerson (he wore those bottom-rimless glasses they put on '50s scientists and FBI agents in the movies), or Shirley Brown (Shirley, I'll *explain*). I have written no plays except the deliberately distorted Tennessee Williams snippet. I have had no outsized breakdowns, just the steady march unto desuetude. But more than occasionally I have thought about that giant, purple, friendly snake, and I have walked the woods looking for one. At first everywhere, anywhere, because they were alleged to be everywhere, and later in rarefied, special terrain, because they were supposed to be there, I walked the woods looking for an indigo, the gentleman snake.

Many parks in Florida have information kiosks with colorful enamel signs showing the special flora and fauna in the park. The gopher tortoise, the scrub jay, the indigo snake. At no park with an indigo snake on its kiosk signs could I find an indigo. If I asked rangers if anyone had seen one, no one had, or maybe someone had, some time ago, and where is that fellow, well he's not here anymore. I finally realized that the thing had gotten so rare that professional help was necessary. If I was to see one of these snakes in the wild, alive, while I was alive, I was going to need professional help. (It is not easy to see one *not* in the wild. The Jacksonville Zoo still has one, and I wonder if it is related to the 1964 snake; I was recently surprised to see one in the Nashville Zoo.)

How a Friendly Old Redneck Becomes a Fool for the Indigo

About the time of the snake play in Jacksonville, Fred Sulley was working construction in an early development of Orlando called Bay Hill and began noticing indigo snakes and realizing they were being displaced by the habitat destruction. "They had nowhere to go," Fred told me. He began taking some home and turning them loose in his house. One, a male he captured at three feet who grew to eight feet, whom he named Big Guy, took up behind the sofa. "That was his place," Fred said.

When friends came over and sat on the sofa, scooching it into the wall, Big Guy would "get mad" according to Fred and could expand and inch the sofa back out away from the wall with the people sitting on it. "They thought it was mechanical and I would say oh no, I got a big snake back there, and they would laugh. Then Big Guy would smell their shoes and pants to see where they had been, like a dog, and come out and raise up about four feet to look at them. Whenever that happened I never saw those people again!" Fred says, laughing.

He credits Big Guy with exceptional intelligence. "Once I came in and put a bucket of KFC down and went to change clothes and when I came back the chicken was all over the floor. My lady friend at the time—Doug's sister—said we should throw him some chicken to see if he would catch it. We had been throwing him mice and rats. He caught them and he caught the chicken too.

"When I would come in he would smell my boots and pants to see where I had been—I had been in the woods all day.

"A friend brought over a husky puppy and I told him to keep it away from the sofa. It went over to the sofa and Big Guy clamped down on its foot and we had to pry him off. They took the puppy to the vet and his foot was broken. They can bite hard."

It's been fifty years and Fred Sulley, whom a friend of ladyfriend-at-the-time-Doug's-sister calls "just a friendly old redneck," still misses Big Guy, who came to an end at the other end of the spectrum from the perils at Bay Hill. "Indigos," Fred says, "are affected by insecticide. All the snakes I had died of colon cancer. I had a roommate that had the place treated for bugs every month. Big Guy was smarter than any cat I ever had."

Doug and Phyllis, who visited Fred and Doug's sister in those days at Fred Sulley's, report having still very specific memories of sitting on the moving couch. They are among the friends who did not run away.

How a Snake-nut Becomes a Fool for the Indigo

A snake enthusiast calling herself snakemama posts this on PetTalk!:

I held an Indigo snake at a reptile expo about . . . nine years ago, and that twenty seconds changed my life . . . I HAD to have one.

They're very unlike any other snake. First, they are unable to unhinge their jaws in order to engulf large prey, so they have to eat smaller prey items. Second, they have a FAST metabolism, so they eat (and poop!) frequently. He eats three or four small prey items a week. Third, they are smart. Grendel clearly recognizes me from any other person, and whenever I am in the room with him he keeps his head out, watching me. He doesn't watch my husband or anyone else.

He's incredibly docile, until he senses food. Then he becomes a maniac! He's also beautiful, as you will see, with big glossy black scales and an enchanting red face. He's very expressive too. He makes little "huff" sounds of disapproval when I'm not taking him out of his tub fast enough or when I won't let him go climb out of my reach.

It took me nine years to get an Indigo snake for a few reasons. They are protected. There are several states where you can't have them at all without a permit, and if you want to get one from any state aside

from the one you live in you need a permit.
They are harder to care for than the aver-
age snake. I clean up after him more than I
clean up after my other snakes all combined.
They get large. He has almost outgrown the
enclosure he is in, and as soon as I'm moved
in a few weeks' time I will be purchasing
a much larger enclosure for him. Mostly
though, they are EXPENSIVE. A newly
hatched baby may easily run over $1,000. I
got very lucky, and an online friend of mine
was putting out feelers trying to find a good
home for this guy. I got an incredible deal
on him.

Here he is [photographs not available]
on the day I received him. I try to leave
snakes alone for at least a week after they
have been shipped to me, but he came out of
the shipping box and crawled straight into
my arms, so I allowed myself a few minutes
to adore him before I put him away.

Here he is a week later, during his first
"real" handling session.

We got used to each other quite quickly.
I DO have to let him know that I'm coming, if I surprise him by taking him out too
quickly he'll strike at me, but if I take it slow
he's completely fine. Soon, I started taking
him out to climb trees!

In the wild, male Indigo Snakes may patrol quite a large territory, so I make an effort to get him out for lots of stimulation and exercise every day.

These snakes will eat ANYTHING they can get their mouths around. In the wild they eat a lot of rattlers and other snakes, but they also eat fish, birds, rodents, lizards, and anything else they can! This has caused me some problems . . . like the day I tried to wipe some spots off the side of his tub with a paper towel . . .

It can also be funny, like last week when I decided to offer him a bite of my pork chop and see if he liked it.

I have let snakemama go on because, as dubious as what she says may look to the non-snake-nut, *everything she says is accurate and true.* She can be called a snake-nut if we may concede that the term is not always pejorative. It isn't.

How a Child Who Becomes a Doctor Becomes a Fool for the Indigo

Linda Perangelo, a retired physician who grew up in Kershaw, South Carolina, not a snake-nut and not a friendly old redneck but a person of sound Duke Medical mind, as a child was handed an indigo snake at a reptile farm in North Carolina. "It was the first snake I had ever held that I did not drop." She had dropped the garter snakes and blacksnakes handed her in Kershaw by her father. "They had just been too frightening. They wiggled and blacksnakes will bite you." The indigo, also black, and easily ten times the size of the lesser snakes, entranced her. She recounts this to me fifty years later, having held the one specimen the one time. "It was my gateway snake."

Strippers Were Fools for the Indigo

Before international trade made the python and the boa constrictor available, if you were a woman in the United States who wanted to remove your clothes and move suggestively for entertainment purposes, and you wanted a snake in your act, you wanted an indigo. It was huge, agreeable to your business, provocatively mobile, and its indigo iridescence, next to your white flesh, in the case of Kathryn "Zorita" Boyd, was striking.

I Had Better Define Snake-nut

It would behoove were I to define the term *snake-nut*. At bottom, a snake-nut is a person who has the chase gene, defined here by Jennie Smith in *Stolen World*, her book about illicit reptile trade: "Levy, like Molt and the rest, possessed the gene that had caused him to chase after reptiles since he could walk . . ." The person with this gene may chase all reptiles, some reptiles, or be a hard-core snakeman only. He, or she, may have the gene only recessively; she may be a botanist, say, with a casual delight taken in the reptiles in the bushes. There are good snake-nuts and bad snake-nuts. Here is a bad snake-nut, again from Jennie Smith: "Bob

Udell was a free agent now, roaming back and forth to Florida, returning with trash cans full of indigo snakes that he kept in his apartment."

A bad snake-nut trading in indigo snakes is one of the historical forces that has depleted the indigo to the edge of extinction. They were beautiful, they were friendly, and they were money. In scientific parlance, "Collection of Eastern Indigo Snakes for exhibition purposes and the pet trade probably contributed to population declines in some areas in the past, and although illegal collecting still occurs, its impacts on populations are probably minimal compared to those of habitat destruction and fragmentation." Note the two probablies. A man in pursuit of the indigo today, seeking professional help, must be careful what kind of snake-nut he appears to be.

As a boy I was a member of a club run by the famous reptile showman Ross Allen, and the club sent its members pseudo-scientific papers mimeoed on construction paper with a three-hole punch. When I read that efforts to force a rainbow snake to regurgitate in order to study its diet killed the rainbow snake, I realized a herpetologist, if that's what it took, I would not be. So my chase gene came to override my study gene, if I'd had one. I merely wanted then, and want now, to hold a snake, not make it throw up, or cut it open, or sell it. I am a good snake-nut.

Turning Oneself In to Professionals

I began by running into an old friend working in herpetology and telling him that I was on my see-an-indigo-before-I-die quest. He told me there were two beautiful women doing indigo research in south Georgia and that I should hook up with them. Indubitably, I said, I want to hook up with two beautiful women who will to boot put me on an indigo. The friend was to send me a contact email. I waited.

After a year I ran into him again. Waiting on the— I said. It's coming, he said. Again it did not, and it dawned on me that this was all just possibly a bit too *Odyssey* to be true—two beautiful women, in the woods, were going to show one an extinct, purple, snake.

I wrote to a writer I know, John Lane, with whom I once hunted snakes in the rock quarry near Spartanburg, South Carolina, where the marble for the South Carolina State House was quarried, and who had introduced me on that trip to David Scott, the most prominent reptile photographer for the state of Georgia. If John knew David Scott, he might know enough to hand me on. John wrote to a Chuck Smith at Wofford College; Chuck Smith wrote to me: I should contact Chris Jenkins, boss of an outfit called the Orianne Society, which, incredibly, is dedicated to preserving the indigo snake. As improbable an idea as an organization dedicated to saving a snake is, that it is, in this case, a *society* is perfect: a gentleman snake belongs in society. This is a society snake if there ever was one.

I wrote to Chris Jenkins from within the Orianne website and heard nothing. I waited. The note I sent was lost, the way those intra-website notes seem to always be, or maybe I had not managed to come off as a good snake-nut. An organization saving the virtually extinct indigo snake might have a significant problem with, and be hypervigilant for, the bad snake-nut. How to let them know I had held one snake in 1964 and was still haunted by it, and that I had no experience with trash cans full of indigo snakes?

I essayed one last go. Just in case they had received the letter from the website to the website, as it were, and it had spooked them, I trod lightly:

> Dear Chris Jenkins:
>
> I've been referred to you via John Lane and Chuck Smith. I asked them where might I best stand a chance to see an indigo in the wild.
>
> I wrote you earlier, to the Orianne site, perhaps going astray, and thought I'd try again. I am pondering, have been for years, doing a piece, possibly long, about the indigo snake as it perhaps symbolizes the peril of all things good in the world we have ruined. . . .

Perhaps itself a bit spooky.

But Dr. Jenkins responds:

> Padgett,
>
> I apologize if I missed your last email. I have ccd Heidi Hall and she can coordinate with you on the best way to get into the field with our staff to see an indigo. . . . [W]e

would potentially welcome someone writing an article about the snake or our organization and again Heidi would be the best person to discuss that with.

Heidi Hall! Does that not *sound* like a beautiful woman? And she is in fact in Georgia working with the indigo. I am back in the *Odyssey*.

And Heidi writes:

> If you could give me a range of dates you would be willing to come out in the field I can start coordinating with our staff. I noticed you are in Florida. . . .

And I write to Heidi:

> I am indeed in Florida. I will be anywhere anytime there is a particle of indigo in the area. . . . I am also just finally determined to see an indigo again outside of a zoo. Orianne might be interested, if you keep an archive of this sort of thing, of a photo of me holding indigo in a book called A WORLD UNSUSPECTED that Duke put out about twenty years ago. I was twelve, then a young fool for the indigo. Now I'm an old fool for indigo.

And Heidi writes:

> Everybody should be a fool for indigos! We
> can do this several ways. We can get you
> into our facility in Florida . . .

And I am not only in the *Odyssey*, I am in the door. I have
presented the credentials of a good snake-nut. I do not miss
Dr. Jenkins's note of caution: "We would *potentially* welcome
someone writing an article . . ." I'll be on probation.

Captive Propagation of the Extinct

It should be noted that I am about to witness animals that I
deep-down have believed extinct for nigh on fifty years. In
my empirical view, they *are* extinct. I know that they are not,
but they still are.

Before I go outdoors to see them, I go indoors. The facil-
ity in Florida that Heidi has invited me to is the Orianne's
breeding compound outside Eustis. The kennelman as it
were is Fred Antonio, with whom I talk for a bit, again presenting some credentials. I show him a photo of me with the
Jacksonville snake. The photo is forty-eight years old when
I show it to him. I have nothing else as a *bona fide*. Fred is not
demanding. We enter a building marked Quarantine. It is
for ascertaining that animals introduced into the breeding
program are pathogen-free. It is fair to say that I lose my
bearings even before I begin seeing the snakes. The floors
are concrete with a spectral speckled epoxy paint on them

that squeaks of clean; the balance of the room is stainless steel and good lighting. It's the kind of place you want to live in and you would if you had serious money. We approach a steel rack of plastic drawers and Fred opens the top drawer and removes from it an indigo snake about eighteen inches long, a hatchling, and hands it to me. Into the silence I proffer, he says, "Isn't that cool?" For several reasons, some of which can be articulated, later, it is. I manage to say "Yes." The snake is, for one thing, a homunculus, a scale model of an adult. Some snakes have the cuteness in the young that characterizes mammalian young—large eyes, delicate body, undeveloped features. Not these. Full-on adult snake in miniature, a bold, strong, confident little purple thing. Secondly, it represents extinction that quite clearly is somehow making little ones of itself. It rocks my world. Fred shows me two-year-olds, four-year-olds. We migrate to a breeding building. He shows me yellow rattlesnakes in drawers, bred from albino stock—"The correct terminology is 'amelanistic partial albino,'" Fred tells me, "but most call these color morphs albinos"—calm, beautiful, canary-yellow snakes. (Orianne also is protecting the diamondback, which does not enjoy federal protection but is probably as imperiled.) He shows me large indigos, one confiscated from a trailer in Ocala with no surrounding habitat for the game wardens to release it in. A pine snake, also protected and rare. More indigos; we go out in the sun and photograph them; I try to reproduce the photo of me at the Jax Zoo. We go back in. At a cage a gravid indigo is in her laying box with her head just out of its hole watching the room.

When we approach she does not draw into the hole. Fred hands her to me. I get a vibe unlike any I've gotten so far. She is not anxious to be put down. Nor is she content to find herself against a warm body, to stabilize and sit tight as a constrictor may. Nor is she crawling to get out of a tree she somehow can't get out of, the position taken by many snakes. She regards me, regards Fred, and thinks at least this: "Hmmm." I say to Fred, "This is a thinking snake." Fred says "Yes." He has known me not an hour, I have shown him an article I wrote with a picture of me and a snake in it. He does not know that I am insane or not insane. He sees that I am right about this snake, because he knows this snake.

We return her to her cage, she re-enters her laying box as any snake would; she circles within it, as any snake would; and she extrudes her head and rests her chin again on the bottom edge of the hole in the box to resume observing the room, as any snake would not. A *dog* would do this, not a snake.

If you pick up a dog and hold it, it seems to think, I don't know why this is happening, exactly, but it is A-okay. That is why I told Fred the snake was a thinking snake. It thought precisely that, pretty much.

All of my suppositions and impressions about indigos formed by the snake in 1964 that bit Mike Wilkerson after the play turned out to be not inaccurate. When Fred handed me the snakes in the lab, fifty years later, I felt I already knew how they move and think. It is fair to say that an indigo snake leaves a lasting impression.

Seeing Extinct Snakes Outdoors

To see the extinct outdoors is a bit harder than seeing them indoors. You have to go into the habitat that is now so famously lost, degraded, and fragmented: "xeric Longleaf Pine sandhills of Georgia where Gopher Tortoise populations are present," xeric upland habitats of south Florida. In the north of this range the snake makes what is called obligative use of gopher tortoise burrows, in the south non-obligative use. In the winter in Georgia the snake can be found near a gopher burrow if there is sun. In Florida the snake is not confined to burrows for its refugia, one of the favorite words in herpetology. It will range into "lower and wetter habitats": "pine flatwoods, hydric hammocks, hardwood swamps." What has degraded, destroyed, fragmented these terrains is a hurricane of forces: logging when we had forests in the 1800s, fire suppression once the original forests are gone, agriculture large and small, urbanization, and pandemic silviculture (putting 700 trees on an acre where 70 once stood). Between these fragments of terrain are roads—an indigo is a huge target and has a lot of himself or herself to get across slick asphalt. To the lay eye, the snake wants some dry ground with some tortoises on it or near it. Usually a pine tree about. Some sand. Some peace.

I am turned over to Dirk Stevenson, the chief field wrangler for Orianne, who came down to the Okefenokee as a child from Illinois and was photographed with an alligator and his mother beside the family car and his chase gene metastasized. He has caught, marked, and recaptured indigos at last count 418 times for Orianne (257 individual indigos).

Offered less by way of credential than I gave Fred Antonio, he agrees to take me afield with an enthusiasm only a
man with a metastasized chase gene can show. "Please let
me know what you think and if this remains a good plan, I
am excited, we shall herp as few grown have." "Let's plan on
you arriving on the afternoon/eve of the 9th and we'll herp
like fools on the 10th and 11th." "I am sure looking forward
to draping a 2 m Dry about your person." (A "2 m Dry" is
a six-foot-plus indigo, *Drymarchon couperi*. The herping tribe
likes Latin and likes to use it, often in coded and satiric ways
making fun of Latin, and of people who use Latin. "Harry
Greene is very interested in where and when you filmed the
horridus footage, if you are willing to share.")

Dirk takes me on a tour that includes a private tract
of land under Orianne's managing help and two conservation easements. It is May and I am told not to expect
an indigo, because we are beyond the obligative-use period of the gopher burrow. I don't expect to see one since
I am now convinced they are vestiges in a laboratory only.
We see beautiful land, hill and dale of good longleaf pines,
and dozens of marvelous golden-sand burrow aprons with
no snake on them. Driving a jeep trail beside a fence line
we see a flash of something that looks metallic—I think it
might be a bicycle fender—and as I realize it is a coachwhip
snake Dirk has ratcheted the truck into park and we are out
of it and I try to go through the fence where the snake is
headed, into a pasture, where I think he will open up and
run like a greyhound, and Dirk with a limp that owes to a
knee or a hip I've not asked about runs back down the fence

line, behind us, I think to get through the fence better than I have, because I am hung in it, completely, and Dirk comes limping back with the coachwhip coiled in one hand and offers it to me. Running this snake down is to my mind not unlike Will Smith's running down the cephalopod or whatever it was that qualified him to be a Man in Black. Moreover, the coachwhip, which I had thought to be a biter, is in a happy docile set of loops about the size of a ladies' handbag when Dirk hands it to me. I begin to think maybe this guy knows what he is doing. If he can run that snake down—it's the fastest there is, here—and charm it into a neat limp nine-inch coil and hand it to a person, maybe he *can* drape two-meter *Drymarchon couperi* about a person. The realm of possibility tilts.

At the conservation easements we join some other her-pers, a term I use loosely and don't like at all. We join peo-ple who want to walk around with Dirk and maybe find an indigo. I begin to see a certain ethos among these people, who more loosely might be called conservation-inclined naturalists and scientists of one stripe or another. There is an ethos among them that a proper man should know what everything in the woods is. En route to a snake, if that is the target, he identifies the plants, the birds, the trees, the soil, the rocks. "Mostly just ride, soaking sun, picking out warbler and vireo song, as Jim boats us to check and bait traps."

Frankie Snow is a botanist at South Georgia College in Douglas who seems to know what everything is, and walks the woods in neat pressed jeans with a marvelously yellow magnolia walking stick and a quiet, wise air. He is the definition of the man with a small chase gene delighted to find a snake in the bushes that he is studying. (I am an amateur, ignorant of every plant and bird in the woods, stumbling on the rocks, after the *snake*. Dirk is in the middle.)

With eyes out for indigo, Frankie Snow delivers a running commentary as we walk, pointing at plants. "Deerberry is a blueberry," he says. "Galberry is a holly." He cocks an ear: "Bachman's sparrow." We pause, listen to the sparrow, resume. "That *Isoetes* there"—he points too vaguely for me—"is the rarest plant on site." I am dumbfounded, if that might mean foundered on one's own dumbness. Suddenly Frankie Snow says something that means something to me: "We've counted nine individuals right here."

"Nine *individuals*? Do you mean *indigos*?

"Yes."

"Nine? Right here?"

"Yes."

They would know it is nine individuals because each would have been marked with a microchip, called a PIT tag. Frankie Snow, with his beautiful yellow stick, his nice blue (non-camo) pants, his soft-spoken all-knowing of the ground and the air, is not jiving me. I begin to hyperventilate, just a bit, ready to stumble on the rocks.

No snake is seen.

An Indigo Blitz in South Florida

People are invited to the Archbold Biological Station east of Arcadia, Florida, to participate in what is called an Indigo

Blitz. The purpose will be to capture two specimens the right size for radios from the failed subdivision developments north of Archbold. These will have the last of Javan Bauder's two federal radio permits installed in them, the radios not the permits. This will give him a total of two dozen snakes radioed up for his population viability study, which is to constitute the fundament of his dissertation, a thing he hopes to be able to do. By my lights a dissertation is an improbable thing even before its execution is predicated on locating live, extinct animals. (And Javan is appropriately nervous; he will one day tell a group of us that the freezing and overcast weather, which will guarantee that we will not see an indigo, nonetheless constitutes "a good day for the sheds to be out." A fresh shed, from the right place, is as valuable for DNA analysis as is a live snake. He is so desperate that we go out that no one laughs at him when he tells us the sheds will be out even in this weather.

Archbold Biological Station is so out there, so intact and pristine-feeling and starlit and big, that you get a frontier-Florida feeling and want to call people and tell them you're there. "And?" they'll say. "And nothing—I'm here. It's . . ." It will do no good to convey the weird sense of things, the pastures and the scrub feeling like Seminoles ought still be on it, the small slate-shingled houses for the researchers that feel forties-made and that Archie Carr must have stayed in, if not Audubon or Bartram.

Dirk and a field man named Andy Day who does population surveys for Orianne come in from a trip they made that day near the Everglades. They have a Florida king snake they found on rocks beside a canal; it coils on my left hand and we type email together for two hours. A king snake is not a thinking snake, beyond what is necessary.

They have found something else. They saw some vultures working something on the edge of the road and Andy said to Dirk, "Let's go see the indigo those vultures are eating," and they stopped and saw that the vultures were eating an indigo. It is a freshly dead extinct snake, the closest I've come yet. It is over seven feet long and the carcass is so voluminous and mutilated and grisly it is hard to look at. It is valuable DNA. A man could easily weep a little looking in the cooler at this bloody mess.

I go out with Javan and his radio man Patrick Barnhart to find nine of his two dozen radioed snakes on the third day of the blitz (no indigos are being found where Javan wants them found). We go initially into some very heavy palmetto cover about truck-high. Patrick is in heavy-duck Carhartt bibs, which he needs. The first snake, Naja, is found, underground. It takes a good half hour to locate her. The second snake, Angelo, is also found underground. The process is to use a non-directional antenna until a signal is secured, switch to a directional antenna, wade into this distressingly heavy cover toward the signal, lower the gain as the signal strengthens, and finally, by a series of signal-here, no-signal-there passes with the antenna at the ground, to determine, with reasonable conviction, that the snake is right here, under you. Temperature of the air and ground in sun and shade are taken, GPS coordinates, all entered into a log, the GPS data later plotted out, providing a tidy home-range overlay graphic for the particular snake on an aerial map. The indigos at Archbold have home ranges ranging from 59 to 1,360 acres and you can see on the aerial map where they roam and forage and mate and sun and bed down. After Naja and Angelo we head for Rambo, snake number three, over in the southwest part of the compound.

En route we are called to another group of hunters near where Rambo is. They have caught an indigo—in fact, Chris Jenkins has. I see my first one alive and not in a lab or zoo. It is adult, but not huge. We head for Rambo, get another phone call. The bastards have found another one, a hatchling. We go back and see it. Ass-chapping. I see now the snake is extinct to me, not to others. I get it.

We arrive finally at Rambo turf and while Javan and Patrick are getting the gear out I head on out to where they tell me we are going. It's a grassy road going down through a shallow creek; on the left of the road is a very improbable highway-grade guardrail. A barbed-wire fence is running along the road on the left, too, becoming one with the guardrail. Why a real guardrail would be on one side of a ranch jeep track on land that has not even been a ranch for a good while . . . and suddenly I am aware that the ground more or less under my feet is rumbling and black, black rumbling is moving and moving fast down this incline along this fence coming to this guardrail, and without seeing it well I am moving too, fast, with this damned indigo snake, no doubt about it, its black blurred presence now shearing under the barbed-wire fence to the left and heading for the creek, and I am too, and can't get over the fence, and can't get over the guardrail *and* the fence, and the snake gets in the creek, makes a hard left turn, goes up the creek for ten feet and into a copse of palmettos on the bank. This took about five seconds. The palmetto rhizomes emerge from and turn back into the bank like giant snakes themselves, a metropolis of thick rhizomes like elephant trunks in mud. The snake needs one hole and these rhizomes provide fifty. I am hyperventilating a lot. Were I going to have a heart attack from excitation, I would have had one right there. We hunt the area for a bit but we are fools to bother. Three of these extinct snakes a quarter mile from each other! The one we *don't* get, mine! A highway-grade guardrail!

Rambo is located underground. Venus (she was caught *in flagrante delicto* with a male named Sigma on Christmas Day) is located aboveground, moving; we see only a foot-long section of her for a tenth of a second in a part in the grass she is porpoising through at a burning speed (we would not have captured a radioed snake anyway). We locate, all underground, CSC, Homer, Marge, Sigma, and late in the day the ninth snake, Betty, so named because she crawled up into a Ford when she was initially captured.

Extinct to me has set in with some teeth. I want to see one of these snakes and catch it. Can it happen? I leave the radio team and go with Dirk and Andy in their truck back to camp. We are flying along beside a railroad track, 40–50 m.p.h., decent sand maintenance road. Andy, sitting sideways facing the rider's side of the truck in the little half-seat thingie of the Tacoma, says, in a serious tone I'd not heard from him, "Got one." Dirk slams on the brakes. I open my door and step out, thrown into the door as happens when you step out of moving cars, and begin running back to where Andy must mean if he said Got one when he saw one. The snake is on a patch of sand the size of one half of a ping-pong table. The other half of the ping-pong table is grass, a patch of grass not more than six by four feet. The snake raises its head and looks at us coming, holds the look just a second, and then *whips* its head away toward the grass and goes. I land on the snake in the grass softly so as not to hurt it but can't feel anything to pin. Andy goes to the farther half of the patch and paws it in the same flat-palming way, covering the area with replacements of his hands and whole forearms, as a cat might. He has gone beyond where I saw the snake. I know I jumped *right on* the snake. I assume he will get it, and that he has gone where the snake was not because as a pro he knows something I do not. *Extinct to me.* Dirk is cutting himself in the palmettos, where the snake cannot have gone; it's too open and clear (not dense like those we faced with Naja and massive like those at the creek), and they begin right beside the ping-pong table, and we'd have seen even a small snake go in there. A giant black snake the girth of a motorcycle tire and over six feet long has disappeared from an area the size of a ping-pong table, one half sand, the other Bahia grass not a foot high. About an hour later, after we issue all the postmortems we can issue, Dirk says she went into a hole under the grass and that we could have dug her out but it would have taken an hour. I have seen three indigos this day, aside from the two slow ones somebody else caught. The ones I have seen are the fastest and smartest snakes I have ever seen. But I have seen them. They are not extinct.

Back at our slate-and-linoleum research pad, like an old Florida lake house, Andy Day says that there are two camps of "herpnerds." (A better term, if more pejorative, than *herper*.) One is the wild, I'll-grab-anything daredevil; he tends to be lean and have stories about where he's gone and what he's been bitten by. The other camp is the sedentary collector, the breeder, who is typically not lean and who talks about the color phases he is making in his breeding. I would add a third category: a boy or girl with the chase gene who has upgraded into science to ratify or exculpate his or her penchant for chasing snakes (or lizards or turtles or frogs or salamanders). This camp tends to be able-bodied, quiet, lean or not, an air of wisdom accruing depending on how high up into the scientific world he or she has climbed. We get abstract in the starry air of Archbold, with grisly DNA in the cooler and still speculating on how that snake humiliated us like that. I am grateful to have seen that snake do to these two pros what the snake at the creek and guardrail did to me alone.

The adult indigo Chris Jenkins captured that day before I failed to capture mine is "worked up"—that is, sexed, measured, weighed, and PIT tagged. The sexing involves inserting a stainless probe into the cloaca. In theory, the theory of the humans doing it, it does not hurt. When this snake gets his/her probe in, he/she bites Patrick Barnhart the radio man, who is holding the non-relevant end, on the thumb. Unlike Mike Wilkerson, florid Patrick does not flinch. He takes it as a scientist should. A small trickle of blood issues. When the probe is removed, the snake releases his grip on Patrick's thumb, and has no more quarrel with it, or with anyone, just as the Jacksonville snake in 1964 had no more quarrel once the security hazard was removed. The snake being probed at the blitz I believe just needed a bullet to bite. No one present knows it, but I am working on a hypothesis myself. If an indigo must bite a human, he will bite on the thumb.

We Finally Get Real

Dirk takes me to some known ground near Ludowici, Georgia, not in May but when it is supposed to happen. It happens. We come up on a slash pile with a burrow more or less into the side, or edge, of the slash pile. We are about twenty feet away yet and Dirk points out an indigo on the slash pile, sunning. "There you go. Go get her."

The snake is on this pile of logs and limbs and stuff becoming, you know, *peat*, and she is facing, and not far from, a cliff of sorts in the pile of logging detritus that drops off sharply, and growing up this cliff are prodigious very thick blackberries. If she crawls just six inches she will be in heavy briars, inextricable. She can probably just enter the very slash pile where she is without moving anywhere. I don't know why she has not already disappeared.

"No," I tell Dirk. "If you need that snake, you better get her yourself."

"You sure?" It has been a year at least that Dirk has been trying to drape a Dry about my person, and this disappoints him. I think the disappointment of my losing this snake for him will be greater, and I see no way, given what I have seen, that it can be captured by me.

Dirk clops as ungainly as a man can clop across the face of this pile of trash, moving logs under the very snake, which continues not to move, so that I am beginning to think this surely a dead snake, and he finally gets there and picks her up, and looks at her face closely, and says, "Yep, just waking up." Her name is Stacey. This is her third or fourth recapture. She is doing well. I'm a little miffed. These Georgia snakes, as Cleve Dean of Pavo, Georgia, once put it in a way different context, is way yonder different from them Florida snakes. The next one is mine.

It is mine, but it is not next. I see one caught by the half party that goes the way Dirk and I don't go one day, a big female that one of the two women on the trip, who has never held a snake at all, wants to hold all day until its release. On that trip Dirk and I hunt a burrow, lying down to look for tracks, as one does, a few feet from a diamondback, which we don't see, but which another person finds, calling us back to the hole to show us how astute we are. I survey hundreds of gopher burrows with Andy Day, going to hundreds of burrows via GPS waypoint, without seeing a snake, or even a tortoise. But I must say: once you get a taste for the longleaf pine and wiregrass, this may be the best futility on earth. I think this is the serenity I saw in Frankie Snow.

And one day, I do not now know where, Dirk and I put in a long day, and at the end of the day, no snake except maybe a diamondback he saw but I of course did not, Dirk saw a track in a burrow and we hunted the area very hard. With a good exit track an indigo should be within a hundred yards of the burrow. We hunted this half acre for an hour. It dazed us. I was becoming glazed with disappointment. We had the ground, we had the conditions. Even I could see tracks by now. We wandered off a bit done-for-the-dayish onto, I think, some property adjacent to where we were actually supposed to be. It was not grand woods. Planted pines. A burrow or two. Dirk calls me from the burrow I'm scoping to the one he's at. He's about ten feet from it. I come up, can see the apron, stop. Close enough to see the area, not too close. "I might be mistaken," Dirk says, "but I think there's a *Drymarchon couperi* in the *Vaccinium*." There is something silly in his attitude that tells me this is not just pranking. There is nothing on the ground around this apron other than a low reddish bush that looks like thinning hair on a redheaded aging man. I can see the scalp through it. I get closer. There is nothing in the bush, but Dirk is standing there like a bird dog on point that has not lifted a leg or gone rigid in the tail. I get between the burrow and the bush, nearly over it, and where there was nothing in this thin bush there is a six-foot bluish snake nervously calculating relocation. I check the broader area: nothing but some thin pine straw for thirty yards, no holes, no palmettos, no briars, no ping-pong tables of innocent grass. There is hardly anything on the ground that would allow for *traction*. This snake has only one option.

I put my foot right in the mouth of the burrow and kneel down on one knee. This is called blocking the plate. I can get up just in case he does try to run. Even if he does he is

going to slip on the straw. Even if he is as fast as the Florida
snakes and does not slip on the straw, he cannot outrun me
for thirty yards. He knows all this and I know it. I have a
goat-herding stick from Kenya with me. It is thin and nicely
finished and light and strong. It was hard to fly home with
it from Kenya because of, yes, 9/11. I get a little Ebola-
memoiritish just thinking about Africa and my stick. But
I got it home, and keep it with me in the field, and with it I
touch the *Vaccinium* gently just to supply a joule of nervous
giddyup to the situation. It's a herding stick after all. The
snake advances a foot or so, his head clear of the red bush,
and looks at the expanse of flat ground with the straw on it.
It's thirty yards before even a small pine tree. He advances
yet, still straight, not turning to the hole but going around
it, more or less, until I put the stick on the ground ahead
of him, and he goes ahead and turns, calmly, inevitably, for
the hole, and as he passes my outside foot and comes to my
knee I pick him up with my left hand and put down the stick
in my right and get that hand on him too for support, and,
after looking fifty years for my extinct snake, it has crawled
right to me. And I see that I have a style: I will not rush an
indigo snake if I do not have to. You do not knock the door
down and handcuff a reasonable man. You ask him to come
into the station, and he will.

Can a Snake Be Saved?

I witnessed a man in a physical-therapy clinic, told by the
cute young women trainers having him do light-barbell
curls that they wanted him to get stronger, ask the women,

without guile or menace, "Can an eighty-year-old man *get* stronger?"

I would like to ask, with the same want of cynicism, can a snake *be* saved? Or is it the case that an effort to save a snake would be the very most hopeless effort in the entire lost world, the lostest of lost causes that has left us our mostly ruined planet? Had I not been haunted for fifty years by this snake I would not ask if it can be saved.

What if the proposition were put to us that we could save at least our part of the world if we could save this giant, purple, friendly snake? Would that be any less absurd than suggesting we could save the world by saving the elephant, or the tiger? As it happens, Orianne was initially funded by the same party who funded Panthera, the foundation trying to save the big cats. The creation myth for Orianne (a myth that happens to be true) goes that Tom Kaplan's (of Panthera) daughter Orianne said, more or less, Daddy, if you're saving the tiger you ought to save this great purple friendly snake, too, and Daddy decided to try.

Proposing saving the elephant or the tiger in order to save the world might be a shade less preposterous than proposing saving a snake in order to save the world, by which I mean that a few more people might get in the game to save the elephant than would get in the game to save a snake. It happens, though, that the game to save the elephant is not going well. It has brought us, we are told, to the slaughter of 25,000 of them a year for their two big front teeth. That does not bode well—the unforgetting, majestic, circus-employable, Dumbo-inspiring giant who mourns its dead and whose prehensile monstrous wiry-haired nose even children want to touch we cannot save to save our lives. How would we purport to save instead a snake, in a world of people who fall into three camps vis-à-vis snakes: the only good snake is a dead snake, a snake is all right if it stays over there, and snake-nuts?

It's a fair question, and only a snake-nut would pose it. But as Randy Newman said of Lester Maddox, this snake is *our snake.* This is our elephant.

The author acknowledges invaluable help from the Orianne Society, Dirk Stevenson, and Andy Day in the field pursuit of the indigo.

Acknowledgments of Previous Publication

Cleve Dean
"Grappling with a Giant: Meet Cleve Dean, Mightiest Arm Wrestler of Them All," *Harper's Magazine*, 1996. "Grappling with a Giant," *The Best American Sports Writing 1997*, George Plimpton, ed., Houghton Mifflin.

Hitting Back
A World Unsuspected, Alex Harris, ed., UNC Press, 1987.

Juan Perez
"A Sausage Run with the Band," *Oxford American*, 2013.

C. Ford Riley
"Realism Reflected: The Natural World of Artist C. Ford Riley," *Garden & Gun*, 2008.

Bill Wegman
"Family Camping," *Hello Nature*, William Wegman, Delmonico Books, Prestel, 2012.

Don Barthelme
Remarks from the Dedication of the Donald Barthelme Papers, University of Houston Library, April 15, 2005. "Come Back, Donald Barthelme: A Symposium," Justin Taylor, ed., *McSweeney's*, 2007. "On Donald Barthelme," *A Manner of Being*, Annie Liontas and Jeff Parker, eds., University of Massachusetts Press, 2015.

Flannery O'Connor
"Craft Talk Without Craft," delivered at Columbia University, 2010.

Grace Paley
"Not Knowing Grace Paley Well," *The Massachusetts Review*, 2008.

Lena Padgett, Nan Morrison
"Padgett Powell," *For the Love of Books: 115 Celebrated Writers on the Books They Love Most*, Ronald Shwartz, ed., Grosset/Putnam, 1999.

Denis Johnson
Tribute read aloud in New York City, 2017.

Spode
"Ode to Spode," *Literary Dogs & Their South Carolina Writers*, John Lane and Betsy Wakefield Teter, eds., Hub City Press, Spartanburg, SC, 2013.

New Orleans

Unpublished, 1992. Commissioned by *The New York Times Magazine, Part II: The Sophisticated Traveler.*

Bermuda

"Paradise Proper," *Garden & Gun*, 2012.

Gumbo

"The Lunacy of Gumbo," *The Artists' and Writers' Cookbook*, Natalie Eve Garrett, ed., Powerhouse Books, 2016.

Squirrel

"Using the Squirrel God Gives You," *Lucky Peach*, 2014.

William Trevor

"Padgett Powell on William Trevor, a Postscript," *Book Post*, September 3, 2018. "Padgett Powell on William Trevor," *Book Post*, May 25, 2018.

Peter Taylor

"Padgett Powell on Peter Taylor," *Book Post*, 2018.

Saving the Indigo

"Tangled Up in Indigo," *Garden & Gun*, 2015.

PADGETT POWELL is the author of six novels, including *The Interrogative Mood* and *Edisto*, which was a finalist for the National Book Award, and three collections of stories. His writing has appeared in *The New Yorker, Harper's Magazine*, and *The Paris Review*, as well as in *The Best American Short Stories* and *The Best American Sports Writing*. He has received a Whiting Award, the Rome Fellowship in Literature from the American Academy of Arts and Letters, and the James Tait Black Prize for Fiction.